ABOUT THE BOOK

In this fascinating book you find that there is a perfect pet for everyone. No matter where you live or what your life is like, you are sure to find at least one favorite among the many different creatures described by the husband and wife writing team of Francene and Louis Sabin. Did you know that crickets and ladybugs can make interesting pets? The authors tell you how to select, house, and feed such loving pets as canaries, rabbits, hamsters, guinea pigs, gerbils, goldfish. The Sabins, authors of the continually popular *Dogs of America*, point out that not everyone can care for a dog or cat in his home. So here you can learn how to enjoy turtles, finches, frogs, salamanders—even ants, earthworms, and other entertaining creatures of land, water, and the air.

PERFECT PETS

By Francene and Louis Sabin

G. P. Putnam's Sons, New York

PHOTO CREDITS

Ewing Galloway: 43, 69
Grant Heilman: 12, 14, 16, 19, 28, 31, 37, 60, 63, 79, 94, 101, 105, 108, 110, 114, 119
Frederic Lewis: 24, 39, 40, 50, 86, 112

LIBRARY OF CONGRESS CATALOGING IN PUBLICATION DATA

Sabin, Francene. Perfect pets. Includes index. SUMMARY: Suggestions for selecting and caring for such pets as canaries, rabbits, gerbils, turtles, salamanders, frogs and others. 1. Pets—Juvenile literature. [1. Pets] I. Sabin, Louis, joint author. II. Title. SF416.2.S2   636.08′87
77-12598   ISBN 0-399-20626-4

IN MEMORY OF FLUTE,
THE MOST PERFECT PET OF ALL

Contents

Introduction

There is a legend that tells this story. The Great Spirit called together all the small creatures of the world and said, "I have brought onto the earth tall, two-legged creatures, to be my caretakers of the lands and the waters. They are strong and wise and possess great powers, but without you they are not complete. Each of you, therefore, will have a job, a special role in this world. Now I add one more thing—that you be friends with these new beings. For they will need your love and the beautiful gifts that each of you can bring to their lives."

And so, the legend concludes, the insects, the birds, the fish, and all the other small creatures of the world agreed to follow the wishes of the Great Spirit. As it was then, so it is now.

The union of people and animals has worked out wonderfully well. In every civilization pets have brightened the homes and the lives of children and grownups. Dogs and cats have been especially popular, and they do make excellent pets. But so do a host

9

of other animals. In many instances, a small, gentle, easy-to-care-for creature makes a better choice than a dog or a cat. Some of us are allergic to furry creatures. So, when we want to bring pets into our homes, we can turn to birds, fish, reptiles, insects.

Other people, who live in small apartments, don't have room for large or very active animals. But a gerbil cage or a fishbowl doesn't take up very much space. And for those people who don't have much spare time, or can't afford the expense of a large animal, or who are physically unable to care for it, this book offers a world of choices.

There is a perfect pet for everyone. Indeed, no matter where you live or what your particular life is like, you are sure to find at least one favorite among the very different creatures described in this book. Whichever one you decide to take into your home and your life will reward you with countless hours of pleasure and satisfaction. For, in the words of the Great Spirit, their role is to be your friend.

1
Smallest Pets

Every spring a miracle takes place. As the trees and shrubs begin their yearly display of green, thousands of tiny creatures suddenly appear, flying, crawling, climbing, buzzing. . . These are the members of the insect world. Of course, they have been there all the time, hiding in the ground, on tree branches, and in, on or under thousands of other secret places. Why didn't you notice them during the cold months? Because they were either hibernating or they were still eggs waiting to hatch in warm weather.

Some of the insects around us are not the kind you would want as pets. The mosquito, for one, has a necessary role in nature but is a pure pest to man. The bee, which helps to pollinate flowers, can be kept for its honey-producing talent by experts. But it takes special conditions, protective clothing, and a great deal of knowledge for the beekeeper to remain safe. And cockroaches, although they are very clean insects despite their appearance, should not be kept as pets. One cockroach will give off an odor that will bring an army of other cockroaches into your house. And nobody in his right mind wants a house full of cockroaches!

Caterpillars, Fireflies, and Crickets

There are lots of insects that make interesting and harmless pets. Most of them are short-term pets, creatures with brief life-spans which should be released into nature at the end of summer. In some cases, they should be freed even sooner. For example, caterpillars, which are easy to collect in the spring and early summer. You can learn about nature by watching them grow and change. But then, one day. . .

Let's begin at the beginning. When you see a caterpillar, gently take it and the leaf or branch it is on, and put them in a glass jar. Then punch a few holes in the jar lid, and cap the jar.

This caterpillar will emerge from its cocoon as a moth.

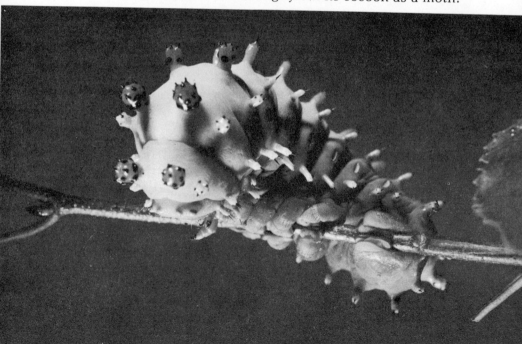

There is no problem when it comes to feeding a caterpillar. Just supply it with more of the food it was eating when you found it. If the fuzzy fellow was discovered on an oak tree, place a couple of fresh oak leaves in the jar every few days. But take care not to set the jar in sunlight—that will raise the temperature too high for the caterpillar to survive.

One day, when you look in the jar, the caterpillar will be gone. Has it escaped? No. Look closely and you'll see a cocoon attached to a branch, or rolled in a leaf. The caterpillar has built this house around itself. When it emerges from its silent home, it will no longer be a caterpillar. It will have become a moth or a butterfly, and should be released immediately into the outdoors. Butterflies and moths cannot live in a limited area.

Just about every young person knows the words of the song that go, "Glow, little glowworm, glimmer, glimmer." And just about every young person has wanted to capture several of these light-producing beetles, put them in a glass jar, and watch them glimmer all through the night. It's all right if you want to do this, but be fair to the glowworms—also called fireflies and lightning bugs—by releasing them the next morning so they can return to do the work for which Mother Nature has created them. And how does a firefly earn his keep in the world? By keeping gardens and other green places clean of slugs and rotting wood.

The light that flickers on and off is a firefly's chemical signal lamp, and is one of the mysteries of nature that scientists have been trying to solve for many years. What scientists do know is that fireflies use these light signals to attract each other during mating season. Their signals work perfectly. As if by a Morse code of their own, male and female fireflies always get their message across to the opposite sex.

Each species has a different code. The common North American male firefly flashes his signal for a split second every six seconds. If there is a female of the same species in the neighborhood, she will signal back with the same timing. That acts as an introduction, and they soon pair off. Other species have different codes—such as a double flicker, followed by a few seconds of no light, another double flicker, and

The firefly on the right is a male, on the left, a female.

so on. Fireflies glow best on warm, humid nights in midsummer, and that's the best time to collect them. Remember, though—they are just on loan for overnight amusement, then back they go into their natural world.

The musical talents of the cricket have endeared them to humans for centuries. Long ago, in China, crickets were favored as pets purely for their singing. They were housed in special bamboo cages in millions of homes. You, too, can have a pet cricket, but a wire-mesh cage will do quite well in place of a bamboo one. (A description of how to build a wire-mesh cage may be found in the section on ladybugs.)

Crickets, sometimes called katydids, produce their singing sound by rubbing their wings together the way a person will rub both hands together. The cricket has a scraper at the edge of its left forewing, and a fine-toothed file vein on the bottom of its right forewing. When the two wings overlap and the scraper rubs against the file vein, sounds are created. Like the firefly's light, a cricket's song is a mating signal. But, unlike fireflies, crickets may be kept for a few weeks in the summer. However, you have to feed them. What kind of food? Just about anything—a bit of meat or vegetable or grain. They are not "picky" eaters.

Crickets are fascinating in many ways. If you have an American tree cricket and a watch with a second hand, you will be able to figure out the temperature of the air. If you have the same cricket and a thermome-

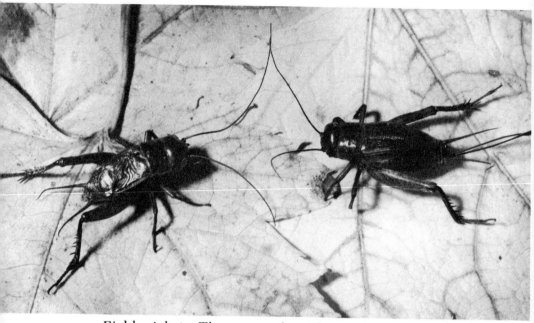

Field crickets. The one on the right is a female, on the left, a male.

ter, you will be able to use your small friend as a timer. The reason is, the American tree cricket speeds up its chirping as the temperature rises.

Using your watch, count the number of chirps your cricket makes in fifteen seconds. Add the number 39 to the number of chirps and the total will give you the temperature in degrees Fahrenheit. (If you want proof, check your answer against the reading on a thermometer.)

Now, if you have an American tree cricket and a thermometer, here is how to use your pet as a timer. Multiply the temperature by four, then subtract the number 160. The result will be the number of chirps your cricket will give off in one minute. Knowing this, you'll be able to boil a three-minute egg to perfection. Be sure to give your timer a bit of the egg as a reward.

There are three kinds of tiny animal pets which can be kept for more than a few weeks. These are the ant, the ladybug, and the earthworm. (The earthworm, while it is not an insect, is close in care and feeding to insects, and for that reason has been included in this chapter.) All three are harmless, intriguing to observe, and of benefit to people. And all three are well worth the time and interest you give them as pets.

Ladybugs

"Ladybug, ladybug, fly away home," we say, taking care not to harm the bright, spotted insect. Even very small children seem to know that the pretty little ladybug (or ladybird) is a friend which should be protected. Indeed, of all the insects in the world, the ladybug is probably man's best friend. It doesn't sting or bite us, it doesn't eat our crops or our flowers. What it does do is destroy aphids, those plant lice which ruin so many green growing things. That alone makes ladybugs worth protecting.

Ladybugs make nice, though temporary, pets. Of equal importance is the knowledge that breeding them is a very good way of helping to keep our world free of harmful pests without using chemicals. So, if you want to keep some ladybugs, start by preparing an insect cage.

To do this, you'll need two pie plates of the same size (any kind will do, such as the disposable ones which hold frozen pies). Then, take a piece of metal or plastic screening, about 18 x 24 inches, and roll it to

17

form a cylinder 24 inches long. One open end of the cylinder should fit snugly inside the inner lip of one of the pie plates, and the other open end will be capped the same way by the other pie plate. When you are finished fitting the plates to the cylinder, your ladybug cage will look like a long can made of mesh, with solid ends.

Now the mesh cylinder must be sewed, or it will unroll. But before you start sewing, clip together the overlapping ends of the mesh at the top, middle, and bottom of the cylinder. The clips will hold the cylinder in shape while you sew it. (Paper clips will do the job.) The sewing can be done with a coarse needle (the kind used for sewing yarn) and string. Begin by sewing the ends of the cylinder very firmly, or, if you have a stapler, stapling them. Then sew the rest of the seam, so that it is securely closed. If you don't, your pets will be able to squeeze out of the cage at the seam and fly away.

Once the cylinder is sewn, fill one of the pie plates with moist soil or sand. Then take a branch with leaves and stand it in the soil. Put the cylinder in place, cover it with the other pie plate, and your ladybug cage is ready to be inhabited.

The best kind of leafy branch to use is one infested with aphids. If it is too early in the season to see aphids on the leaves of a rosebush or fruit tree, take the soil for the cage from the ground under the bush or tree. The plant lice which live in this soil (and harm plants) will provide a complete diet for your ladybugs.

The best time to go collecting ladybugs is when

they first appear, in the spring. Don't take too many, because overcrowding is not good for them. Besides, we need them in nature to help us keep plants free of aphids. Put no more than six or eight ladybugs in your cage, and place the cage in a warm spot. The only other thing you must do is keep your pets supplied with an aphid-covered branch or infested soil. They must eat in order to survive.

Soon after the ladybugs are used to their new home, they will probably lay their first batch of eggs on the branch. And within a short time larvae will hatch out of the eggs. Don't be surprised at these ugly little creatures—ladybug larvae don't look anything like their neat, glossy parents. The larvae also don't need their parents, so it would be a good time to release the adults, freeing them to do their work in nature.

Ladybugs are not only pretty, they help to destroy insect pests.

The larvae—black little crawlers with thick bodies and six legs each—will, in three to five weeks, be fully grown into a new adult generation. And all through their growth they will be happy to eat as many aphids as you provide.

In the weeks between birth and adulthood, the ladybug larvae will go from being tiny black bugs to somewhat larger black bugs with colored spots on their spiny backs. Then, at last, they will change into the pretty ladybugs with which we are so familiar. To do this, of course, they must first change from larvae to pupae. This change is something you will enjoy watching. The larvae weave a little case on a branch, settle into it, and will finally emerge as adults. This transformation into an adult beetle involves a shrinkage of the outer pair of wings to a bright, spotted shell. The shell, by which we recognize the ladybug, consists of these two outer wings. When the ladybug flies, it lifts the shell, exposing the thin under-wings, which propel it through the air.

The ladybug has two defenses against predator enemies. One is that bright, hard shell. It acts as a shield, the way a turtle's shell does. The other defensive weapon is the bad smell the ladybug gives off when it is crushed. (It probably also has a foul taste to any bird that attempts to use it as food.) Birds and larger insects, which might otherwise make a meal of the ladybug, seem to learn very quickly that is is best to leave this spotted beetle alone and search for tastier tidbits in nature.

When your larvae have pupated—that is, become adults—release all but six or eight, then start all over again. In fact, you can continue to breed ladybugs until autumn. That's when they stop laying eggs.

Ladybugs go into hibernation during the colder months, huddling in groups that look like small bunches of flowers. If yours do this, just put the cage in a safe place, out of reach of winter storms, and let your pets sleep until springtime. That's when they will begin the life cycle all over again.

While ladybugs are not the kind of pets you can train, they can be amusing to watch. A swing, made of two sticks with a toothpick suspended on a string between the sticks, will be used as a trapeze by the daring little acrobats. What's more, they will use any other form of miniature gymnastic equipment you provide for them. Like busy explorers, your ladybugs will examine anything added to the cage, walking over every part of it, flying and swinging and doing what is natural for them, and what will look like tricks to you. And if you put your hand in the cage, at least one ladybug is sure to take a hop onto your finger and begin walking the length of this new "thing," inspecting it for food or for ways to use it. Don't worry about being hurt—about the only feeling you'll get is a tickly sensation from the ladybug's legs.

If you don't want to breed ladybugs, but just want to keep a couple as pets, that's fine. Simply follow the directions to make a cage (although it can be smaller, since it will be housing a smaller number of ladybugs), make sure there is food available during the summer months, and enjoy your tiny spotted pets. Let them have a long walk now and then along your fingers and wrist, and play with them in any way that gives you fun and doesn't hurt them. And remember, if keeping our environment healthy matters to you, release them in the fall. After all, every ladybug you protect will help to maintain a green and beautiful world.

Ants

When you see ants running across your picnic table, they are just pests that have to be chased away. But as pets, ants are fascinating little fellows. Of all nature's busy creatures, they are the busiest—always working, helping one another, keeping their colony in a non-stop flurry of activity.

It may be hard to believe, but there are 8,000 species of ants that have been identified by scientists. These different species are scattered all over the world. Some are black, some red, others yellow. There are species that gather seed, others that spin out silky threads, still others that live in trees and feed off the sweet secretion given off by other insects. And then there are the wandering army ants, which travel in large groups. Certain ants can even inflict a serious sting, but don't worry—you are not likely to find them in your garden or the local park. The common gray or black ant we find in the United States is absolutely harmless to human beings.

All ants are built just about the same. An ant's body has three sections: the head, the thorax (middle section), and the abdomen. If you look at one closely, you'll see it has six legs, all attached to the thorax. Ants reproduce by laying eggs and, though they often live in the ground, they are air breathers.

Every ant colony has three classes, or kinds, of ants—the queen, the worker, and the male. The duties of each class are very sharply defined, and all are needed for the colony to survive. They live by community effort. To understand how this works, imagine that the whole colony is a kind of living being. It cannot exist without food and shelter, so the workers must supply those for every ant. It must reproduce new generations—baby ants—so the males and the queen see that this need is met. The queen is the only ant in the colony that lays eggs, and she lays hundreds of them over a lifetime that can last many years.

If one of the three classes should happen to disappear (this sometimes happens when nature or other insects damage the colony), the whole colony would die. That is because each class is not able to perform any function except its own. Most animals, including man, perform all the functions of life when they are needed. But each ant, being able to do only one thing (lay eggs, or gather food, and so on), depends on the other classes of ant in the colony to do everything else. Ants, as you can see, are very dependent on each other—and the entire colony—for existence.

Now that you know the basic facts, why not start your own colony? Beginning your own ant nest is very easy. First, find a gallon glass or clear plastic jar with a lid that fits tightly. (There are commercially made ant farms for sale in toy, department, and other stores. These contain everything you need but the ants, which can be ordered by mail. The ready-made

23

farms are fine, but a homemade ant home will serve just as well.)

Let's say you are doing-it-yourself, and you're using a jar. Stand a tall, thin can or a block of wood in the jar. If a can is your choice, be sure it is cleaned after you have removed anything that was inside, then put it in the jar with its open end toward the bottom. Now, surround the can or block with *sandy* soil in which the ants will live. The can or block will keep the ant tunnels from being dug through the center of the jar— completely out of your sight.

The soil should be slightly moist and about half as high as the can or block of wood. You will add more

A queen Carpenter ant (left) communicates with a worker ant.

soil after you have collected the ants, but the soil must never reach the very top of the can. Once the soil is in place, put a damp sponge or a little dish of water on the top end of the can and put the lid on the jar. This will keep the soil moist. Ants do not live in locations that are bone dry or too wet. They need a little bit of moisture, but not too much.

Now is the time for an ant hunt. For that, you'll need two small jars with caps, a piece of cardboard, a sheet of white paper, and something for digging—a shovel or trowel will do fine. The best place to begin your hunt is under a rock in your garden or the park—anyplace where the soil is soft. Lift a rock and look underneath. If there are lots of ants scurrying down into holes, you've found the site of a nest. Quickly remove the cap off one of your jars, and brush the ants into the jar with the cardboard. If the ants disappear before you can collect more than two or three, release the ones you caught and start looking for another nest. Never mix ants from two nests in your ant farm; they will only fight and kill each other.

When you have succeeded in collecting a large number of ants from one colony, cap the jar and put it aside. Now you want to find a queen ant from the same colony. She lives beneath the soil's surface, deep in the nest, so start digging. You may have to dig as much as a foot into the soil before you reach the inner part of the nest, where the queen breeds.

Turn each shovelful of soil and ants onto the white paper. Mixed in with the many small ants will be one that is much larger than the rest. This is the queen. Gently guide her into the other jar, and cap it. Then take the two jars, your equipment, and some of the soil from the nest. Your hunt is over, and you're ready for the next step.

Of course, you may have encountered a problem— being unable to find a queen. Well, you still can have an ant colony. For one thing, the other ants may produce a new queen. That happens sometimes, though not often. But, even if it doesn't, a colony without a queen can live and function for many months. However, the colony will cease to exist when these ants die and are not replaced by a new generation. With a queen, of course, you can keep the colony thriving for years.

Here is how you transfer the ants to their new home. Set the jar in a large pan of water. This helps to keep a daring ant or two from getting away, which has been known to upset a human parent or two. If a clever ant does manage to crawl over the side of the jar while you're putting in his colony-mates, he will crawl down the side of the glass, reach the water—and run right back up again. Ants cannot live in water. By some method of communication which scientists have not fully solved, the ant that ran back from the water will let the other ants know there's an "ocean" down there.

Before putting the ants in their new home, re-member to add some of that soil you brought from outdoors to the soil already in the gallon jar. Press it down gently. The soil should be loosely packed, and no higher than an inch from the top of the block or can.

The last ant to join the colony is the queen. Open

her jar and very gently direct her to her new home, keeping in mind that the colony's long life span depends on her survival. Once she's in, put some food on top of the soil. What kinds of food do ants eat? Pretty much anything—crumbs of bread, bits of meat, dead insects, pieces of leaves or vegetables. Just scatter a small amount on the soil's surface and cap the jar.

Once this is done, wrap a piece of black paper or black cloth around the jar, fastening it securely with tape or rubber bands. Ants build their tunnels and nests underground, away from light. By wrapping the jar with a dark cover, you can recreate that environment and make the jar a suitable place for tunnel building. Next, put the wrapped jar in a warm (over 85° would be *too* warm) location for a couple of days, and let the ants become accustomed to their new home.

When you want to see how things are going with your six-legged pets, unwrap the jar. The subsurface soil, you'll discover, will be woven with interconnecting tunnels and passages. You may see one ant or a group of them pulling some food from the top of the soil down into the nest, while others may be moving eggs or young larvae from one part of the nest to another. You may even see the queen feeding the larvae. Ants being ants, there should be great activity and lots for you to see.

Every few days check the condition of the food and water supply. Before adding fresh food, remove any left over from the last feeding before it rots. Keep the water dish filled or the sponge wet. If the soil seems

An ant colony with its interconnecting tunnels.

too dry, put a few drops of water directly onto the surface. And if you place a stone on the soil, you will see that your ants will move their "front door" to be directly under it. (Remember, they were living under a rock outside.) Then, in a day or two, come back, move the stone, and see what happens.

With very little trouble and periodic care, the ant-colony-in-a-jar can survive for years. Just don't forget to wrap the jar when you're not watching the ants in action, and keep the soil moist and the food fresh. That way you—and the ants—will be very happy.

Earthworms

Fishermen call them "night crawlers" and use them as fish bait, but you can make true pets out of crawly little earthworms. They're called night crawlers because they are most easily found at night.

During the day earthworms prefer to stay in the ground, shoving their way through the soil. They come up after sunset or when the day is very cloudy and dark, so that is the time you should go looking for them. Earthworms come up to feed on leaves, grass, and bits of plants, which they either drag back into their underground burrows or eat on the spot. The other thing that brings them up is moisture. An earthworm likes moist, but not wet, soil. That is why, in the summer, you may see many earthworms on the ground after a rain. Birds know this, too, and do their most successful worm hunting on wet lawns.

If you would like to establish a worm colony, you should know a few simple facts. Besides being unable to live where it's too wet, earthworms cannot exist in total dryness, in direct sunlight, or in extreme cold or heat. Summer's burning sun sends them to cool, moist places. Winter's frigid air sends them deep into the ground where they remain curled in burrows till spring. Earthworms don't hibernate the way bears and other animals do, but they do stay underground and scarcely move all winter. During this time they keep alive on stored-up food.

Before you start collecting earthworms, have their home ready for habitation. All you need to begin with is a large, wide-mouthed jar or plastic container. You may also use a box or can, but it's more fun if you can watch your pets digging along. Thus a clear-sided container is better than a can or wooden box.

Fill the jar with a mixture of loose soil and sand. The aim is to give your worms a home like the one they would choose in nature. Worms do not like hard, dry clay or wet mud. The best environment for your colony would be the soil in which you find the worms.

If your jar holds about a gallon, you will be able to house comfortably up to a dozen worms. If the jar is smaller, bring in fewer worms. In any event, before you gather your pets, have the jar filled with soil and be sure the soil is moist.

Night or a dark day is the easiest time to find worms, but you can also find them on a sunny day. Look under rocks or leaf piles, or dig down into soft ground to find a burrow.

The worm-filled soil and any free worms you turn up should be placed on a folded newspaper. Be gentle in handling them; earthworms are easily injured. Carefully separate your worms from stones and other debris you don't want to keep. Then place them in a can or box with some leaves or grass. Keep in mind that direct sunlight kills them, so they must not be exposed too long. As soon as you have collected six to a dozen fat, good-sized worms, bring them into the house or cellar and transfer them to their permanent home.

When the earthworms are first placed in their jar, they are probably going to rest a while. This is the way they adjust to their new environment. Soon, however, they will begin to tunnel down into the soil. If you put the colony in a cool place overnight and come back in the morning, don't expect to see even one still on the surface. If one does remain on top, it may mean that it isn't healthy and should be removed from the colony. Don't take any chances. You can't be sure how it will affect the other worms.

Feeding earthworms is very easy. They like fresh and decaying leaves. Though they are not fussy eaters, their taste preferences are interesting. While earthworms may go for a particular variety of leaf when it is fresh and green, they may not like it much when it decays. Yet another variety may be more to their taste when it is decayed than when it was green.

Here is how to find out just how your pets feel about different leaves. Whenever you place leaves in the jar,

A common earthworm.

make a note of the kind (oak, willow, beech, maple, and so forth) and whether it is fresh or decaying. Cover the leaves with a damp cloth and set the jar in a dark, cool location. Then check on what's taken place in a few days. Some of the leaves should be gone from the surface of the soil. Those are the ones your pets have pulled down into their burrows. The leaves remaining on top should be thrown away, after you have identified their kind and condition. You will now know which leaves are not to your worms' tastes.

Though the little wigglers are perfectly happy living on leaves, you may want to vary their diet. Just remember that earthworms are vegetarians and do not eat meat. Give them some grains of baby cereal, salad greens, a bit of fruitskin or bread crumbs. Then see which should be added to their menu. It is important that you don't put too much food in the jar or it will spoil before they can eat it. About one tablespoon of food a week is right for a dozen earthworms.

At first it may be hard to tell which end of a worm is the head and which the tail. After a while, however, you'll notice that one end looks more pointed. That is the head. The other end, which is somewhat flattened, is the tail. One section of the adult earthworm which looks a little different is the saddle, or clitellum—a thick section about one-third below the head. Thus, to tell the difference between head and tail, find the clitellum.

Worms lay eggs. When they do, the clitellum slides off the worm to become a cocoon for the eggs. Then tiny baby worms hatch from the eggs and burst out of the cocoon.

Just as worms have a front and back, they also have a top and bottom. Put one of your pets on a piece of paper. If he turns over, you will know that he is righting himself. Take a magnifying glass, and study the side he has turned to the paper. (Of course, you'll have to turn him over first.) Notice the little bristles on his underside. Every segment of the worm, except the first and last, has four sets of these bristles. The worm uses them to help himself move through the soil, as if he had many small, digging hands. He also uses them to hold onto the soil in case a bird tries to pull him out of the ground.

When a worm is resisting a bird's pull by holding the soil, the worm may break in two parts. Or maybe a piece of a worm was separated from the rest of his body when you were gathering your colony. This doesn't mean that the worm definitely will die. If the break is between the head and the saddle, and close to the saddle, both pieces will become whole worms. The head part will grow a new tail, and the tail part will grow a new head.

If the worm breaks in two between the saddle and the tail, probably only the half with the head will become a full worm and grow a new tail. The half without a head or saddle may grow another tail and become a worm with a tail at each end. However, it will not live long in that state. In any case, nature has made up for the worm's fragile construction by giving him the ability to grow new parts.

You may want to put some cut worms in a separate jar of soil as an experiment. Put the jar in a cool, dark place for about a month. Then check the contents and discover something remarkable. You will find that your injured pets have repaired themselves.

You can perform other experiments with your friends of the earth. Place one on a sheet of damp paper or a damp cloth. Turn out the lights in the room. Now shine a flashlight on the worm and watch his response. Switch off the flashlight for a minute. Then turn it on again, holding your fingers over the lens so that only a sliver of light touches the worm. You will find that the worm moved away from the bright light, but crawled toward the dim light. Worms have no eyes, so what made him respond to the light? He "sees" it with special sensitive cells in his head. Now that you know this, shine the filtered light at different parts of the worm. See how he turns his head toward it? Clearly, he doesn't need eyes to sense the light. Plants respond to light the same way. It is called being phototropic.

Try different color cellophane sheets placed in front of the flashlight lens. Your worm will react differently to each color light. Fishermen often use red flashlights when they hunt for worms at night. Why are they more successful with those than with a clear light? Think about it—the answer is in an earlier part of this section on earthworms.

Worms also respond to sound, even though they have no ears. When one or two of your pets have come up to the surface of the jar, gently thump the soil near them or the side of the jar. The worms will pull back into their tunnels. Their sensitive bodies feel the vibrations made by the thumping, and they react as if they are hearing it.

You can also find your own proof that worms prefer moist soil to dry soil. Fill a large jar or fish tank with soil and put a piece of heavy cardboard or plastic in the middle. This divider should reach down until it is one inch from the bottom and should stick out above the surface of the soil. Place your worms on the surface with the same number on each side of the divider. Sprinkle some water on only one side of the divided soil. Continue, every day, to water the same side of the tank. After a week or two dig up the soil on both sides. You won't be surprised to find more worms on the moist side, since you know they prefer moist to dry soil.

There are many other simple experiments you can do with your colony of earthworms, using simple mazes, different size leaves, colored lights, foods, and sounds. Treat these delicate fellows with the care and respect you'd give any living thing and you'll have a colony of silent, busy pets.

2
Birds

There are two types of birds which can be kept as pets. One includes finches, canaries, parakeets, mynahs—that is, all birds prized for their talking or singing abilities, and housed in indoor cages. The other kind includes ducks, pigeons, chickens, geese —all birds which are better housed outdoors.

Chicks and Ducklings

Usually pet chicks and ducklings enter our lives as Easter gifts. They are small, sweet, and charming, but it is cruel to the bird and its human master to try to make an outdoor creature a housebound pet. So, unless you have a garden and neighbors willing to put up with your raising "barnyard" animals, return them to the pet shop immediately.

Why immediately? Because you'll fall in love with the adorable creature right away, and soon find yourself with a half-grown chicken or duck which will grow unhappier and more unmanageable each day. Animal shelters are teeming with these dis-

Ducklings are adorable, but these animals should not be kept as indoor pets.

carded pets, and it is a terrible fate for the bird, as well as heartbreak to the owner.

If you do have an outdoor area and the desire to keep an adult domestic fowl, it can be a tame pet, pleased to be a part of your world. On our street, there is a family with two dogs, a number of cats, and a goose. All the pets are restricted to a fenced yard and enjoy perfect harmony. The honking of the goose is a familiar sound in our neighborhood. However, since this book is devoted to the care and feeding of indoor pets, we'll only suggest that anyone keeping domestic fowl call the local U. S. Department of Agriculture Extension Agent for advice on the needs of these animals.

Homing Pigeons

This is another species of bird that must be housed outdoors. They require special housing—called cotes or lofts—as well as a fair amount of care and a great deal of freedom. The freedom may present no difficulty to you or the pigeon, but it can be a definite hardship on neighbors who don't share your affection for pigeons. The problem in that homing pigeons tend to settle on roofs, fences, or any other place near their home base. That means all of the houses surrounding yours. And unless your neighbors like the constant cooing of pigeons and the heavy accumulation of pigeon droppings, you'll have constant complaints. If you want to keep pigeons and think your home conditions are suitable to them, check with the neighbors before you get in touch with a local pigeon fanciers' club. You are certain to find one in every area

Homing pigeons must also be housed outdoors.

of the country; its members can best advise you on obtaining pigeons and how to house, feed, train and care for them.

Indoor birds present far fewer problems, except for members of the parrot family, which we do not recommend as pets, Parrots are beautiful, clever, and amusing creatures. However, they are too often carriers of diseases dangerous to humans. For this reason there are rules against bringing parrots in from other countries. Furthermore, veterinarians warn against keeping parrots, even if they are legally purchased. We second their warning. Do not allow yourself to be tempted to own a parrot. There are a number of safe, healthy, trainable species of birds, and you would be wise to select your feathered pet from among them.

Mynah birds

These birds enjoyed a great surge of popularity in the United States during the 1950's and continue to be among the favored indoor pets today. Then, as now, they were praised for their marvelous talents for talking and seeming to understand everything their masters said. But, in spite of some bird lovers' claims, mynahs do not understand the words they can be trained to say, even though young mynahs are quick to learn to imitate the sounds of human speech.

Talking mynah birds are amusing and interesting pets.

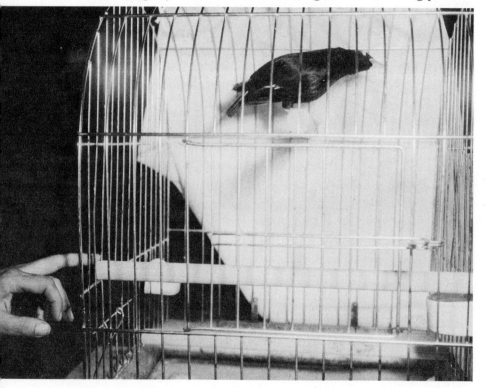

A relative of the grackle and crow family, the talking mynah grows to be nine to fifteen inches in size, depending on the particular species. These black birds will eat everything, and they do well on a diet of fruits, grains, vegetables, and dog food. Just about anything you'll eat, your mynah will eat. But in smaller amounts. And, just as you require a balanced diet to stay healthy, so do they. Remember that a dish of water must be kept in a mynah's cage to be used as a drinking fountain and bathtub.

The joy of keeping a mynah comes from hearing it talk. Every mynah, male and female, can be taught to talk, provided it is young when you start and you give it good care. Just one warning—watch the choice of words you teach your feathered recorder. Once a word or a phrase becomes part of its vocabulary, it is there permanently. And more than one guest has been shocked by a pet mynah bird's salty language.

Canaries

Finches cannot be taught to talk, but they are marvelous singers. All of the varieties of finches available in pet shops make excellent home companions that are a pleasure to both eye and ear. Since the canary is the most familiar kind of domestic finch, the advice for housing, feeding, and caring for the canary is appropriate for all finches.

In the Atlantic Ocean, off the west coast of Africa, is a group of small Spanish islands called the Canaries. Some people mistakenly think that the islands were named because of the birds of the same name. Rather, they were given that name because of the large dogs the Spanish invaders of the 15th Century found roaming the islands. The Latin word for dog being *canis*, the islands came to be known as the Canarias.

Spanish sailors who went ashore in the islands were impressed by the lovely songs of a native bird. Bright green in color and quite small, the bird filled the air with melodies unlike any heard before by Europeans. Of course, the nightingale, with which the Spanish were familiar, sang a beautiful song—but only at night. These island birds warbled, trilled, and chirped all day long, sometimes alone, often in groups like a many-voiced chorus. Small wonder, then, that the Spanish sailors wanted to take them home as pets for their wives and children. And so, in small cages made of twigs, the first canaries were introduced to Europe.

Within a century canaries were popular pets throughout Europe, even though they were still relatively expensive. However, their hardiness and the ease with which they were bred in captivity soon made them plentiful—and inexpensive.

Commercial breeding of canaries was done on a large scale in Germany and Austria. Breeders were interested in developing two particular aspects of the canaries. Their first aim was: produce a pure yellow bird. The second was to produce one with a song similar to the nightingale's. Through years of selective breeding, the green shade of the wild canary was bred out, creating the brilliant-yellow bird we now know as the canary. In fact, the color breeding was so successful that the bird gave its name to a special color: bright, clear yellow is often referred to as "canary yellow."

Canaries will entertain you for hours on end with their song.

The efforts to create a canary that would sing like a nightingale was also successful, though to a lesser extent. There is a type of bird known as a "roller" canary, that sings with its beak almost completely closed and has a song somewhat like that of a nightingale. The roller's song is very soft, and sounds like an imitation of water gurgling in a stream.

Rollers are often bred for singing contests and are trained to begin singing the moment they face the judges. Points are awarded for each song variation, and the bird able to sing the most varieties is the winner. Roller canaries are almost as interesting to watch as to listen to because they look almost like mechanical wind-up toys as they sing through un-moving beaks. Even so, they make fine pets—

although they are usually more expensive than the ordinary canary.

The canary most people know best is the yellow-feathered "chopper." It is called this because its song contains sounds as if the bird is singing "chop, chop, chop." The song is loud and free and not very different from the song of the wild canary heard by those Spanish sailors of long ago. The chopper is a happy singer, a hardy bird, an ideal, inexpensive pet.

Whether you buy a chopper, a roller, or one of the more exotic "show types" of canary, the most important thing to keep in mind is this—buy your canary between the months of October and March. Canaries molt in the warmer months. This process makes them a little ragged-looking. It also makes them more prone to upset and illness. Moving to a new home and new conditions can throw a molting canary off its diet. Also, when molting, canaries do not sing with the same thrilling sound as they do in the winter, so you won't have a fair chance to judge the beauty of the birds' song.

The time to buy your canary is when it is sleek, fully feathered and in full voice. So pick one of the right months, listen to a number of birds, then choose the singer which most appeals to you. Make sure it is a young bird. Canaries can live as many as fifteen years, though a life-span from seven to ten years is most common. These fine-feathered friends begin singing when they are about one year old, and are usually at the height of their vocal careers until they are about five.

You may be able to spot a really old bird by the

scaliness of its legs; otherwise, it is very difficult to determine the age of a canary. Most birds sold in pet shops are supposed to wear a permanent leg band which will tell you its age. So look for a banded bird that is between one and two years of age. It is wise to deal with a pet shop whose owner has a reputation for honesty and whose customers have no complaints about the way he deals with them—and his pets.

You will need a cage to house your new pet. One made of metal or plastic is recommended. There are handsome wooden or bamboo cages available, but they cannot be cleaned as easily. Your cage should have a removable floor tray, and food and water dishes which can be fastened from the outside. These features are for your convenience, not the bird's.

Line the cage floor with newspaper. Sprinkle grit on it, or provide a small dish of grit for the bird. The grit helps the bird digest its food. Birds have no teeth. They swallow grit, which lodges in the gizzard and acts as small grinding stones that break up the food. The only other items necessary for your bird's health and well-being are commercial canary food, an occasional bit of fruit or salad greens, and fresh water.

Some canaries love to take a bath; others don't. Don't be distressed if your feathered singer isn't a bather. Try putting a few snips of green leaves in the bath. This may entice the canary to try the water and splash around in it. If that doesn't work, spray the bird with a fine mist of water about once a week. (A mist atomizer, used for spraying houseplants, is perfect for this.) But do this spraying only if the room is warm—you don't want to give your canary a chill.

If your bird doesn't raise his voice in song as soon as you bring it home, don't fret. It may take a few weeks for the little fellow to get used to his new surroundings. But once he feels comfortable and secure, he'll start to entertain everyone within earshot. There are records which sometimes help, especially with canaries that seem shy and unnaturally silent. These records have canary songs that often inspire a quiet bird to join in. It isn't that the records teach him a song—they arouse a sort of competitive instinct. "You think that's good?" your bird seems to think. "Well, listen to this!"

One canary authority has another suggestion for coaxing a silent bird into song. He says: shake a half-filled box containing wooden sticks or kitchen matches a few feet from the bird's cage. Canaries seem to like the sound and respond to it with a song. Nobody knows why this is so, but it works. And that, after all, is what you're hoping for.

Often a bird that doesn't sing is just a tired bird. Canaries need a great deal of sleep or they'll become ill and silent. The covers made for bird cages serve a very real need. They keep out all light, and mask many of the noises which tend to keep a canary awake long past its bedtime. Cover the bird cage after sundown and do not take it off until morning. Of course, you can uncover the cage now and then at night to show off your pet to a visitor. But don't do it too often. Keep your feathered friend well-fed, warm, and well-rested, and it will reward you with song and beauty for many happy years.

Parakeets

It's a small, bright-colored cousin of the parrot, and it's called a budgerigar in England. What is it? If you say it's a parakeet, you are right.

A cheerful, bouncy, easy-to-care-for house pet, the parakeet calls Australia its homeland. A naturalist first saw this species of bird on that island continent almost 100 years ago. They were nesting in tree hollows, chattering merrily, and behaving like airborne clowns. Australian natives called these enchanting little creatures budgerigars, which means "pretty bird." The name "parakeet" was given to them later.

The parakeets first brought to Europe and America were mostly grass-green in body color, with blue tail feathers. Today, however, they come in all the colors of the rainbow and in any combination of those colors. Which means that, if you want one as a pet, you can pick one to match your room, your eyes, your favorite flower—anything in the spectrum. The most expensive parakeets are white or sky blue because those are the hardest colors to produce in breeding. But if you just want a happy house pet rather than a rare specimen, you'll find a parakeet very inexpensive to buy.

Parakeets are sold at pet shops, by breeders, or at local variety stores. Your best bet is the pet shop, where you'll also be able to get the proper cage, food, toys for the bird, and accessories. Also, the owner of the shop will be glad to give you advice about care of the parakeet. We recommend pet shops over breeders or variety stores because breeders are likely to charge more, since they specialize in parakeets, and don't sell in such large quantities as pet shops and variety stores. Variety stores do not specialize in pet care and consider their pet departments as just part of a large business involving many different products. So they are not likely to be as careful and informed about their pets as the other two dealers in parakeets. And of course you do want to start out with a healthy bird.

If you hope to train your parakeet to talk or do tricks, buy a young one. It's easy to tell a baby bird from a grown one. When it's young, the parakeet has a striped head and is called a "barhead." As it grows, the bird molts, losing the stripes. A very young parakeet's stripes cover the entire head. An older bird will have a solid-colored patch above the nostrils.

Parakeets live from five to fifteen years. Once a bird has lost the baby stripes, it is impossible to tell how old it is. So, if you want to have your feathered friend around for a long time, make sure you start with a baby.

As with many pets, a baby parakeet is much easier to train than a grownup. Old birds which have never been hand-held may act nasty and bite if you try to tame them. That's another reason for buying a baby bird.

A healthy parakeet—the only kind to have—will be perky and active. Parakeets do not normally stay still very long, and you should not buy one that isn't moving around the cage. A listless bird is probably a sick one.

Examine your pet-to-be carefully. Look at his cere

(nostrils). They should be neat, dry, and clean. If the parakeet's nose is running, he's not the one you want. Also, check the condition of his feathers—all over. They should be clean, dry, glossy, and complete. Check for patches where feathers may have fallen out.

Your choice of bird may look fine, except that he lacks the long tail feathers his cage-mates have. That doesn't necessarily mean he's not well. There is a parakeet without tail feathers called a creeper or French molter. For some reason, which scientists do not yet understand, this parakeet does not develop a normal set of feathers. He'll never be able to fly, but is most likely to be a perfectly healthy fellow in all other ways. And if you fall in love with a French molter, there's absolutely no reason not to take him home with you. However, it's probably a better idea to select a normal bird, the kind you'll enjoy watching as he flies around the room and does ceiling-high maneuvers.

Try to pick out a parakeet that isn't finger-shy. This will be one who has been handled by humans a great deal and is used to people. Hand-tamed parakeets are a bit more expensive, but will save you a nip on the finger every now and then. In any case, the bite of a baby parakeet isn't worth worrying about. He isn't likely to even break the skin. So just decide whether the extra cost is worth it, or if you'd rather do all the taming yourself.

Some people think that only male birds can be trained to talk, and only female birds can be trained to do tricks. This isn't true. Males are more often the talkers, and females are more often the acrobats—but

*Parakeets are hardy and friendly pets with a playful
personality.*

not always. Whether your parakeet learns to do
whatever you want to teach it will depend on two
factors more important than which sex it is. The first
factor is your patience. It takes weeks—sometimes
even months—of gentle repetition of a lesson before a
parakeet catches on to what you want. Which means
that most of his (or her) success is up to you.

The second factor is the parakeet's personality. Like
people, parakeets have individual personalities. One
bird may chatter merrily and learn to imitate words,

50

but refuse to do any tricks. Another may be just the opposite. A third may simply be "his own person," and never agree to perform. Yet he, like the others, may still be a delightfully friendly pet. And there is always the possibility that he's a slow learner who needs more patient training.

Even though it doesn't matter which sex you choose for most reasons, you'll still want to know if your parakeet is male or female. The color of the cere will be your clue. Males have blue nostrils, females have brown. These colors, however, do not become clear until the bird is six months old. So if you're buying a baby parakeet and you name it John, you may have to change the name to Joan in a few months. Not that it will upset your bird. After all, a boy parakeet doesn't really mind having a girl's name, and a girl parakeet won't fly through a wall because she has a boy's name.

But you might care. Which is to say: the safest name for a baby parakeet is one that has nothing to do with the sex of the bird, and is pleasing to you. Many people call their parakeets "Pretty Boy" or "Pretty Bird." That doesn't sound very imaginative, but it may be a wise choice, especially because the chirp of a parakeet sounds as if he is saying "pretty bird." Then, when you say it, you are imitating his call. And the familiar sound may attract him, as if another parakeet is calling to him. Bird whistles attract birds on this principle of sound imitation.

Once a parakeet is selected, the next step is to prepare its home. Any standard bird cage will do. The easiest to clean is the kind with a removable tray.

Droppings should be removed daily and the tray washed in hot water before returning it to the cage.

A parakeet wants fresh water every day, a cuttlebone on which to keep his beak in good condition, food, and grit. There are special cups which can be attached to the cage, to hold food, water, and grit. You may also hang a little mirror on the side of the cage and suspend a couple of toys from the top. Parakeets love to look in the mirror and chatter at the bird they see there, and they always enjoy performing aerial hijinks on their toys. As you'll see, a happy, well-cared-for bird is a delight to watch and play with, and a great deal easier to train.

Training should not start as soon as you bring your new parakeet into the house. Let him get used to his new quarters for a few days. Too many new things at one time can be very frightening to a baby bird. So, wait until he seems relaxed and comfortable, then begin his training by letting him get used to your hand. Put your hand into his cage very slowly and steadily. Don't scare him with quick movements, which may seem frightening to him.

Some birds, particularly those that are already hand-trained, will hop right on an offered hand. Others need a little coaxing. Hold your hand as if it were a make-believe gun, with the index finger pointed at the bird. Press this finger gently but firmly against the parakeet's chest. If he bites, do not withdraw your hand. A baby bird can't do any damage to your skin. Just relax and keep your finger in the same place.

If he sees he can't scare you away with a nip, your

pet might not be tempted to use biting as a weapon. And so, as he gets used to your hand and learns that it means him no harm, he'll soon hop on the finger pushing against his chest. If he doesn't—remember, different parakeets have different natures—take out your hand slowly and close the cage. You can try again tomorrow.

After a few days of the same process, if necessary, your bird is sure to catch on to what you want, and he'll accept the finger. Now let him perch a while, move to another finger, become perfectly secure. At the same time talk to him in a soft voice. Keep this up and you'll sense when he is ready to be hand-held outside the cage. When that moment comes, make certain that all the windows and doors in the room are closed. Nighttime is best, in case he flies off your finger and out of reach. All you have to do is turn off the room light and he will stop flying. Parakeets do not like to fly in the dark, and he will sit still until you are able to recapture him. How will you be able to have some light to do this? Use a flashlight.

A finger-tame parakeet is ready to begin learning to talk. This doesn't mean that a parakeet can really talk, in the sense that he understands what he is saying. Birds that imitate speech are merely making sounds they are trained to repeat. In the wild, birds learn calls from other birds. In a human home the bird learns its calls from people. It may sound as if a trained parakeet actually knows what he is saying, but he doesn't.

There are records especially made for training parakeets to talk, but it's more fun to do it yourself. Hold the bird firmly but gently in the palm of one hand. His head should be between your thumb and index finger. Stroke him lightly and let him become calm. Be sure the room is quiet and not too light, and that you are alone. Any distraction to the bird makes learning harder.

Say the word or phrase that you want him to learn. Keep it simple. "Hello there" is much easier to learn than "Good afternoon, Mr. Frogbottom." Repeat the lesson. If the bird is a real genius, he may pick it up immediately. More often it takes weeks, sometimes months, of repetition before the bird gets the idea. Once that happens, though, it won't take long for him to learn new words and phrases. Then the problem will be to get him to be quiet. "Hello there" a hundred times an hour can become a bit tiresome. Then all you have to do is interest him in something else, such as one of his toys or his mirror.

Teaching a parakeet to do tricks depends on the same basic approach—patience and lots of repetition. Suppose you'd like your bird to push a tiny doll carriage. Begin by holding the bird on your finger. Stroke him and talk to him soothingly. Now put the carriage on a table or other flat surface. Place the bird on the table and bring the carriage to him very slowly. When he seems comfortable with it near him, touch the handlebar to his beak. If he backs away, try again. Continue with this for no more than fifteen minutes once or twice a day. It will take many repeats of this lesson before he grabs the bar, holds on and pushes it. But don't be discouraged. Just do it over and over, adding a step after he has learned the one before. Be patient—don't try to teach your bird to do two things at the same time. This will only confuse him, and may make him refuse to try any tricks.

Keeping your cheery chirper healthy is not difficult at all. He should always be comfortable and out of drafts. Parakeets come from a warm climate and cannot take extreme cold. They are also unhappy, and likely to lose their feathers, if their room is too hot. In nature a bird would seek a cool, shady place on a hot day. But since he has no control over his environment, your pet bird must depend on his master to adjust the climate. So keep in mind: coolness but not air-conditioner freezing on a warm day, and warmth but not oven-hotness on a cold day.

Parakeets are very clean creatures and spend much time grooming themselves. A bath may be welcome, too. There are parakeet bathtubs which fasten to a cage. Some birds love it and hop right in. Others—and nobody knows why—just will not take a bath. These non-bathers, as pointed out previously, should be sprayed with water occasionally from a small atomizer—the sort used to spray houseplants.

A parakeet that spends too much time scratching himself or that pulls out his own feathers may be suffering with mites or some other parasite. There are treatments which help, and the pet store owner or a local veterinarian can advise you on what to use and how to use it.

In spite of their weighing only a few ounces and measuring only seven inches, parakeets are really hardy little fellows. Most of their problems are not serious, and often result from over-loving masters. A parakeet may be willing to try any food you give him, and will overeat if you let him. Which means that you must make certain he doesn't eat the wrong things or too much of anything. A bit of fruit or green vegetable once a week is fine, but no more. Even if your bird chirps at you in the most charming way, asking for more, resist the temptation. Even if he doesn't know better, you do. Kind and proper care will keep your parakeet in great shape for many years, and he'll pay you back with a sunny disposition and many hours of play. In other words, give him your love and he'll give you his.

3

Small Mammals

All mammals are air breathers, have backbones, and are warm-blooded. And almost all mammals are born fully formed and their first food is mother's milk. Mammals come in all sizes and shapes. Some are as small as field mice and others as large as elephants. Some are as tall and thin as giraffes, and some as short and stout as hippopotamuses. Some are roamers, who will wander far from their places of birth. Others are content to spend their entire lives within walking distance of home.

The mammals in which we are interested here are those best suited to life as domestic pets. Members of the rodent family—mice, hamsters, gerbils, and so on—are furry fellows who are little trouble and lots of fun to raise. There are two types of rodent to be considered as pets: those that can be captured and brought in from the wild, and those that are more normally bought in pet stores.

The first group, which includes field mice, chipmunks, and squirrels, can be marvelous pets, but we do not recommend them. Unless you are able to obtain one that comes from parents that have grown up in human homes themselves, don't take the chance. Animals that live in the wild may carry diseases dangerous to people. There is nothing wrong with throwing food to squirrels or chipmunks in the park and putting out table scraps for field mice. But taking them into your home is another matter entirely.

On the other hand, gerbils, hamsters, and guinea pigs, which come from a long line of rodents bred specifically for home living, are ideal. They are safe, free of disease, and quick to make friends with humans.

Rabbits

The rabbit is often classified as a rodent. Even though it is not, we will consider it in this group of home pets. Every year, at Easter, hundreds of children are given baby bunnies as gifts. The large-eared, soft-furred, cuddly little rabbits are bred solely for this purpose. These animals are all descended from European rabbits, which have been domesticated for many years. There is no native American rabbit or hare that will survive in captivity for any length of time. So, even though the pet rabbit you see in the store looks like the cottontail you see running around in fields and forests, it's only a very distant cousin.

Before you ask for a rabbit of your own, think about where you live. It is not wise to have a rabbit for a pet if you live in an apartment. An adult rabbit needs a lot of exercise and should be outdoors whenever the weather is nice. If you live in a private home, keeping a rabbit should be fairly uncomplicated. If you live in an apartment, however, you would be better off having a pet that needs less space.

A rabbit should be housed in a hutch no smaller than three feet in length, two feet in width, and two feet in height. The hutch, usually made of wood, is divided into two sections. One section is completely closed, except for a rabbit-sized hole. This hole leads from the closed section into an area with three screened sides. One of these screened sides is hinged so that it may be opened when it comes time to feed your pet or clean his quarters. In a way, a rabbit hutch is like a one-room house with a covered, screened-in porch.

Rabbits are naturally clean. They are easier to housebreak than a cat, which is known for being an especially clean pet. A rabbit will choose a particular spot to place its droppings and will always use that same spot. Fresh sawdust, changed every day or two, will keep the toilet area clean and free of odor. (Straw, cat litter, or cedar chips can be used instead of sawdust.) Straw makes the best bedding in the wood-enclosed section of the hutch, and it will not have to be changed very often. Your rabbit will use the enclosed area as a bedroom, and will be careful not to soil it.

Rabbits are vegetarians. Their basic diet can consist of commercial rabbit pellets, which supply them with all their essential dietary needs. To this, you may add carrots, and some fresh greens such as celery or lettuce. Rabbits also need water, so be sure to keep a

A New Zealand white rabbit mother and her babies.

dish or water bottle available to them at all times. Finally, there should be a piece of salt brick where your rabbit can reach it. This item is available in any pet shop.

The weight of an adult rabbit seldom goes above six pounds. If your rabbit weighs more than six pounds or looks overweight, cut down on its food and give it more exercise. This way you'll prolong your pet's life and keep it in good temper. Another clue that your rabbit has been penned too much is when it tries to bite or scratch you. Remember, it can't talk, and it has to express its unhappiness in whatever ways nature has given it.

The most common reason for a pet rabbit to behave in a nasty way is that it has been confined to its hutch for too long. For this reason, it would be a good idea to build an outdoor rabbit run for your bunny. The bunny run should have wire mesh or slatted wood sides, and should be no smaller than four feet by four feet. If you imagine it as a sort of playpen, you have the right picture in mind. Do not forget that rabbits can hop very high; so cover the top of the run with wire mesh. One more point: rabbits are also good tunnel diggers, which means you should check your pet every couple of hours to see that it is still in the run. Give your rabbit regular airings whenever the weather is not too cold and the ground is not wet. These outings will keep it healthy and in a pleasant temper. After all, who wants a grumpy rabbit?

If your long-eared pet shows any sign of illness— loss of weight, a scraggly coat, diarrhea, paralysis of the legs, or any other unusual sympton—take it to your veterinarian. But don't worry that things will go wrong. Good care and a balanced diet are usually enough to keep this naturally hardy animal in top condition for a normal lifetime of five years.

Hamsters

If you don't have space to keep a rabbit as a pet, you might want to have a hamster. The golden hamster, a desert dweller that originated in Israel, weighs four to six ounces and measures six to seven inches at full growth. It is a very clean, sweet-smelling animal. It can also be a very devoted pet, squealing with recognition when you or someone in your household approach it. But there is another side to this devotion: because hamsters are easily scared, they do not like being handled by strangers and may nip at an unfamiliar hand.

Since you want a tame, pleasant-tempered hamster, do not consider taking one that is more than four weeks old. If you raise it from babyhood with care and gentleness, it will return your thoughtful treatment with trust and affection. It is wise, however, to say "no" when one of your friends wants to handle your hamster. Nature has given the small, vulnerable hamster just one weapon for protection—sharp teeth, which it will use any time it feels threatened.

A hamster's teeth also pose another problem. These small creatures do a large amount of gnawing. So, when preparing his living quarters, remember that a wooden cage is not a home but a challenge to a hamster. Like the beaver, the hamster just naturally gnaws wood and will put its teeth to work on any

This golden hamster has stuffed his cheek pouches with food.

piece within reach. So you should house your new pet in a metal cage or glass-sided fish tank.

By no means are we suggesting that you neglect the hamster's need to gnaw. In fact, see that it always has a good supply of wood. This supply of wood and an exercise wheel are very important to the health and good humor of a pet hamster. Except in the winter, when hamsters hibernate, your pet will be as busy as a beaver all day long, running and gnawing. It's also a good idea to cover the cage's floor with cedar chips. Not only do the chips absorb moisture and odor, they also provide the hamster with more gnawing material.

As much as they love to gnaw wood, hamsters do not eat it. So what should you feed this four-footed bundle of fur? Commercial hamster food will satisfy all its dietary needs. Or, you can prepare its food yourself from dry dog food, some cereal grains, and any raw vegetables available. Even dandelions and fresh-cut grass are fit food for a hamster's table.

Although a hamster may seem to accept every bit of edible stuff you offer, it never overeats. In the wild it would take the food and carry it back to its home. That is why the hamster has those bulging cheek pouches for stuffing in the food to take home. But in captivity it will fill the pouches, empty them into a corner of the cage—and forget about the food it has dumped there. With food being provided every day by you, there is never any need for your pet to go to its reserve stores. So, just keep the cage clean, and don't be surprised to find little clumps of food hidden among the cedar chips in different parts of the cage. Be sure to remove them, however, because they will spoil after a while.

All hamster experts agree that, though you need a male and a female for breeding, it is best to keep just one as a pet. Two hamsters in one cage often results in non-stop bickering—and sometimes serious injury to one or both. It's not because they are natural enemies, or that males don't like females. It's simply that a hamster cage doesn't allow your pets to enjoy the kind of privacy they seek in nature. They like living alone. So, take the experts' word for it and stick with one happy hamster at a time.

Of all the small, furry mammals kept as pets, there are two species most recommendable. These are the guinea pig and the gerbil. Both have the qualities of sweet temper, good health, and simple needs that people appreciate most in pets.

Guinea Pigs

In the world of dogs, there is a breed known as the Alaskan malamute. It got its name from its place of origin, Alaska. In the world of horses, there is the Shetland pony, which originated in the Shetland Islands. Indeed, the animal world is filled with creatures whose names come directly from their places of origin. You might assume that guinea pigs came into being in the country of Guinea, on the west coast of Africa.

But that is not so. Actually this furry, tailless fellow is a member of the rodent family and comes from South America. Then why is it called a guinea pig? To begin with, in South America there is an area called

Guiana. This name, like Guinea, comes from a Portuguese word which means "a faraway or unknown land." Guinea pigs may once have been referred to as Guiana pigs, and then the two similar-sounding place names became confused by people, and Guinea won out over Guiana.

The "pig" in the name is the result of the sounds they make. A hungry guinea pig sometimes grunts. A happy guinea pig sometimes whistles. At other times, a hungry one whistles and a happy one grunts. Now, as everyone knows, pigs grunt (has anyone ever heard a pig whistle?). So, because of the sound a guinea pig makes when it is hungry, or tired, or happy—or just because—we call these furry South American rodents guinea pigs.

And just to make it even more confusing, think about this: guinea pig fanciers, who breed them for show purposes, call guinea pigs by their more scientific name—*Cavia*. Thus, they are also known as cavies. But, call them what you will, they are delightful pets.

Just as some breeds of dog come in more than one type of coat (for example, there are smooth or wire-haired fox terriers, short-haired or long-haired dachshunds), so guinea pigs come in three varieties of coat. There is the English short-haired guinea pig, the Peruvian long-haired, and the Abyssinian rough-haired. Each looks quite different from the others, but they're all the same under the coat.

The most common type of guinea pig is the English short-haired. It is sleek, the easiest to care for, and never needs grooming. A healthy English short-haired guinea pig will keep its coat glossy and smooth all by itself, which is probably why it is the most popular of the three types.

The Peruvian long-haired guinea pig looks like a furry pom-pom when it is not moving. In fact, unless it is eating or moving around, you'll have a hard time telling which end is the front. The Peruvian's hair can grow to be several inches long. It flops over the eyes and ears, and every other part of the animal that might give you a clue as to which end is which.

This variety, though a delight to look at, requires daily grooming. If it isn't combed regularly, the hair tends to tangle and form mats of fur, which must be cut off. (It is possible to comb out the mats, but it takes great patience and time on your part and on the part of the guinea pig.) A daily brushing with a toothbrush—the kind of attention a guinea pig loves—is a much better idea than periodic haircuts.

The third variety, the Abyssinian rough-haired, looks as if it has rosettes decorating its backs and sides. As a matter of fact, the more rosettes it has, the more valuable it is. Eight rosettes are considered just the right number for an Abyssinian show guinea pig, but more are better. The hair itself is coarse, similar to the coat of a terrier. Abyssinians need less grooming than Peruvians, but more than the English. Because of their distinctive coats, however, Abyssinians are usually considered show animals and can be very expensive.

All of the three varieties of guinea pig are available in a wide range of colors—white, black, gray, dark brown, light brown, gold, orange—or in any mixture of these colors. Albinos (all white with pink eyes) are not unusual, and are perfectly healthy. An albino, if it is mated, will produce babies in the normal range of colors.

A full-grown guinea pig weighs about one pound and measures about nine inches from nose to hind end. The best time to buy one is when it is still a baby, just weaned from its mother. This would be at about six to eight weeks of age, when it will weigh eight to twelve ounces. At this age, a guinea pig is a playful, gentle, curious little fellow. It adapts easily to new surroundings, responds well to training, and is very affectionate.

It is not often that a guinea pig will bite, but to be doubly sure of having a very tame one, buy it as a baby and raise it yourself. An older guinea pig that shies away from a human's touch has probably been mishandled by someone when it was younger. Even the shy ones can be trained to trust people, with kind and careful handling, but it's obviously wiser to start with a baby and not have to overcome problems created by someone else's mistreatment.

Your guinea pig's home can be an empty fish tank, a small animal cage, or a wooden box. So long as the guinea pig has some room in which to exercise, a place to sleep, and another place to eat, the home will be the right size. Guinea pigs are clean and sweet-smelling, and a layer of straw, kitty litter, or wood chips will help to keep him that way. These substances are good absorbers of moisture and will keep the pet's pen dry and fresh.

Guinea pigs like to sleep in a cozy den, so put a

small cardboard box in one corner of the pen. A shoebox, turned upside down, with an opening cut out of one of its ends, is perfect. The guinea pig will probably push some of the straw or chips into the box to make a comfortable bed and will require nothing else for happy sleeping. Of course, if you want to sing it lullabies to encourage sweet dreams, go right ahead.

Guinea pigs are affectionate and make delightful pets.

Commercially packaged rabbit pellets make a sound basic food for your furry pets. To the pellets add some fresh greens, carrot pieces, bits of fruit, and cereal grains—but never meat. Guinea pigs are vegetarians, in nature and in captivity. Like humans, but unlike most other animals, guinea pigs are not able to manufacture vitamin C in their bodies. For that reason, it is a good idea to give your pet a bit of tomato, cabbage, or raw potato now and then. (Guinea pigs don't go wild about raw potatoes as much as some other foods, but they'll eat them if there's nothing else to tempt them.)

Because they are nibblers who spread their intake of food over their waking hours, it is hard to tell exactly how much food to give a guinea pig. Also, like people, some are bigger eaters than others. Since your pet can't tell you about his appetite, just put enough in the pen so that it isn't all eaten in one meal, but not so much that the food has a chance to rot. The rabbit pellets, being dry (which means they won't rot), can be given in a large amount. What isn't taken from the dish one day will be eaten in the next day or two. The greens and fruits, however, should be given in small amounts—just enough for one day. Watch how much your pet eats and in a short while you'll know how much is just enough.

Guinea pigs need water, so you ought to make fresh water available at all times. If you give your pet raw carrots and fruits, and do it regularly, your guinea pig is likely to get all the water it needs from them. But again, since your pet can't tell you if it's thirsty or not, it's best to keep a dish of fresh water in its eating area.

And in the summer a dish of fresh water in the pen is a "must."

A special treat, as well as a healthful meal for a guinea pig with a cold (yes, they catch colds just as people do), is some bits of bread soaked in milk. Add a few drops of cod-liver oil, and you have the best possible pick-me-up for an ailing guinea pig.

Like many other furry creatures, guinea pigs can become hosts for fleas. The treatment for a flea-plagued guinea pig is a thorough cleaning of the pen, followed by a dusting of the pen and pet with flea powder. (If the pen is kept clean at all times, the chances of infestation are extremely slight.)

A bath in warm, soapy water, followed by a thorough rinsing in warm water, also helps to keep your pet free of pests. A guinea pig may not adore being given a bath, but it's not likely to protest too much if you are careful and gentle. Part of being careful is making sure that water doesn't splash in your pet's eyes or get in its ears.

When the rinsing is finished, roll your bundle of wet fur in an old towel. It will squirm and rub against the cloth, drying itself. Some guinea pigs really come to love a bath and squeal or whistle when they are in one, as they do when given a favorite food.

Guinea pigs get great pleasure from perching on something while they are eating, playing, or simply resting. A couple of wood blocks placed in the pen provide excellent perching places. Or, if you have an old toy truck (not rusted), you might put that in the pen. Your pet will push it around or perch on it, and enjoy every minute of play or rest. Guinea pigs enjoy playing, which is why they can be trained so easily. Performing tricks, such as sitting up on hind legs to beg for food, or doing a little waltz for a treat, are as much fun for a guinea pig as they are for the person who teaches the tricks.

Use a piece of favored food in training. Hold the food in one hand, above the head of the guinea pig (but within its eye range), while you lift the front of the pet with your other hand. If your guinea pig helps by pulling itself upright, reward it with a nibble of food. If it doesn't help, don't give a reward. Patience and constant repitition will eventually teach your pet to sit up for its treat. When it has learned this trick, go on to "dancing lessons."

How do you get a guinea pig to dance? When it is sitting up, move the treat a little distance away. Now the animal must take a step to reach it. If it does, give the reward. Next time, don't reward the pet until it has taken two steps. Little by little, you will get the idea across. In fact, some guinea pigs begin to dance whenever they see their masters in hope of getting a treat.

It doesn't matter whether you own a male or female guinea pig if you want a peaceful, cuddly pet. Both are loving, both friendly. It is only when you put two together that the matter of sexes becomes important. Two females are fine, a male and a female are fine, but two males can sometimes spell trouble. There are some males that get along wonderfully, but there are some pairs that will fight and hurt each other. Male and female together will never injure one another, but they will mate and may produce more guinea pigs than you want. So, unless you are prepared to house a number of pets, stick to one guinea pig of either sex or two females.

No matter how many living balls of fur you have in your home, you can be sure of one thing—you'll always enjoy having them.

Gerbils

Until the 1950's most people had never even heard of gerbils. A few scientists had studied them in the wild to see how they lived and related to each other and to the world around them. Then during the 1950's, a small number of gerbils were imported into this country for laboratory use. They proved to be scientifically valuable—and lovable. And it didn't take long for these easily tamed, pert little animals to become popular pets. Everything about the furry, friendly fellows made them just right to welcome into a home, especially a home with children.

There are many species of gerbils. They are found throughout Africa, the Middle East, and Asia. Of them all, however, it is the Mongolian gerbil that Americans have come to know and love.

The average gerbil is about three to four inches long, not counting its tail. Some are larger, some smaller. Some have a tuft of hair at the tip of the tail, others have no hair on their feet. And from nose to tail he tips the scales at two to three ounces, is very active, friendly to people, and extremely easy to feed. He's also very easy to please, with food, attention, and things to play with.

A healthy gerbil's fur is thick and shiny. His back

and head are reddish-gold, his underside is white. He has bright, dark eyes, perky ears that react to every sound, long pale whiskers, and squirrel-like pouchy cheeks. Like a kangaroo, the gerbil's front legs are much shorter than his hind legs. In fact, he's related to the kangaroo rat, which gets its name from having long hind legs and the ability to leap great distances.

The gerbil runs on all four legs, but hops and stands on just the hind legs. When he is standing still—which isn't often—he tucks his front paws against his sides and looks like a tiny soldier standing at attention. His front paws are also used as hands, to grasp food, a stick, anything he can hold.

Gerbils are the cleanest of all rodents, and have no odor about them. Because they originated in hot desert areas, they need very little water, and that explains why they produce very little liquid waste. Also, because of their self-cleaning habits, there is never any need to wash or bathe a gerbil. They are fanatics about staying clean and neat. When they aren't playing, eating, or sleeping, they're grooming themselves like people primping for a party. If two live together, they'll groom and clean each other, too. You might say the gerbils' motto is: NEATNESS COUNTS!

Some authorities say that gerbils live about two years in captivity, but they have been known to survive for five or six years. (The authors can vouch for this from personal experience.) They are happy in a tank or cage (we housed our gerbils in a large fish tank), and never feel confined. Like most animals, however, they appreciate having some room to spread out. In nature gerbils live in burrows under the desert sand and never stray far from their homes. Being active creatures, they get all the exercise they need in a relatively small area.

Put a gerbil in a tank with an inch-deep layer of wood chips and an exercise wheel. Immediately, he sets to work rearranging things. He scurries around, carrying chips in his mouth, placing them here, moving them there, stopping every so often to chew them into smaller pieces. Then suddenly he'll take time out to stand still and look around like an architect surveying his latest building.

But standing in one place for more than a moment isn't in a gerbil's nature. So, onto the exercise wheel for a few fast turns. Then off the wheel and back to work. A pyramid of chips is piled in one corner. *Hmmmmm*, the furry builder seems to say, *maybe they'd look better over there.* The scurrying and chip-toting begin again. He turns and kicks some stray chips into place, climbs to the top of the hill, and starts pushing it all away. *Whew! An animal's workday never seems to end.*

But even gerbils take time off, and now's the time, as the busy little creature takes a break for a nap. It's a short one, however, and he cleans himself a bit, decides that his "house" looked better the first way after all, and rearranges it all over again. Like the white rabbit in *Alice in Wonderland*, a gerbil is always dashing about as if he's late for an appointment.

As a pet, a gerbil will be perfectly happy alone or with a mate. Gerbils are quite sociable and do well in pairs or in groups. If you have a male and a female, you'll most likely have more young gerbils by and by. But if you've set your limit at two, there is no reason not to put a pair of the same sex together. The only reason to worry would be if the tankmates are two males who have already mated with females. They might fight and harm each other. With young males, or females of any age, no such problem will arise.

A pair of gerbils living together for any length of time become very devoted to each other. They play together, groom one another, feed from the same dish at the same time, and sleep curled into a ball that seems to have two tails and eight legs. Their pushing, pouncing, and nipping may look like fighting at first. But then they'll dust themselves off from the "battle," and you'll see that it was only friendly roughhousing—gerbil-play.

Except for the drumming of their hind feet to signal danger or some imaginary threat, gerbils are very quiet creatures. They can make a tiny squeaking sound, but usually don't once they are grown up. In fact, squeaks are often the first sign a gerbil owner has that a new litter has been born. The babies, naked of fur, their eyes tightly closed, call for mother with those high-pitched squeaks.

Gerbils are as comfortable breeding in captivity as in the wild. They can reproduce from the age of about one year. They breed anytime from spring to fall and are able to produce litters at the rate of one a month. Each litter will contain one to ten babies. Fortunately, nature has made the gerbil wise to the danger of overcrowding. So if a litter is not taken from the parents, they are not likely to produce another.

The mother gerbil is very tender with her young. She nurses and cleans them, covers them with chips for warmth, and protects them carefully. When she wants to feed or get in some exercise, father takes over as baby-sitter. Gerbils are extremely good parents. Unlike some other animals, who mistreat their young, a gerbil father is never a threat to harm his babies. He's there to provide tender loving care.

A week-old gerbil has a few hairs on its otherwise naked, pink body. These look like pale fuzz on his back. His eyes are still closed, and he still depends on mother's nursing for all his nourishment. But every day brings change—he's getting bigger and furrier and more active. Now, when Mom and Dad leave the nesting area to eat or take a whirl on the exercise wheel, Junior begins to explore his world. He crawls and tumbles this way and that, full of adventure and confidence—and clumsiness. Of course, he's still a baby with closed eyes, and sometimes he gets himself wedged into a corner. Other times he just gets tired and hungry and can't find his parents or brothers and sisters, even though they may be only a few inches away. That's when little gerbil lost sets up a squeaking cry, bringing a rescuing parent to carry him back to safety.

When a gerbil is about three weeks young, he is a perfect physical miniature of his parents. His eyes are open, he runs around and plays, and though still nursing, he tries to eat solid food. He grows more and more successful chomping on the real thing, and within three weeks he is completely weaned. He may snuggle next to his mother and try to nurse, but she knows that he doesn't need to and refuses to baby him. *All right*, she seems to be telling him, *you're a big boy now.* And it isn't a terrible rejection at all. It's exactly what she would have done in the wild, to prepare him to go out on his own. If you decide to keep the family together, rather than give away the young or move them to another tank, all the members will remain playmates and sleep curled in one corner throughout their lives.

Because they are so self-sufficient, gerbils are not in the least bit difficult to keep as pets. All they need is a home, food, and a minimum of care. There are cages made especially for small rodent pets, and one of those is fine. However, a large fish tank is even better. Buy a "leaker"—a slightly damaged fish tank that will leak—at a pet shop, unless you already have an empty tank in the house. Leakers are reasonable in price, since the pet shop owner knows they cannot be used as fish tanks.

The glass-sided tank has a slate floor, which is easy to clean. And its transparent walls allow the pet owner to watch his active friends at work and play. The tank's walls are also high enough so that flying chips won't be scattered all over the floor of the room around the tank. Since a gerbil may arrange his chip pyramid a dozen times a day, the fallout from a cage would become an annoyance. And if there are two gerbils, it would be double cleaning trouble. While one is rebuilding the nest in the far corner, his buddy may be rebuilding it in a near corner. Eventually, they'll settle on one or another arrangement of the "furniture," but in the meantime their mad spring-

Gerbils are energetic little animals who always seem to be busy.

cleaning scatters wood chips here, there, and everywhere. Which is why a covered tank beats a cage every time.

The tank's cover should be a metal one, and it should be available at the pet shop where you buy the gerbils. The cover has rows of air holes, and is expressly made for gerbil tanks. It isn't that gerbils are great jumpers that makes it necessary to cover the tank. It's because they are great builders and climbers. A one-inch-deep floor-covering of chips, when piled in a corner, will reach near the top of the tank. Then all it takes is a small hop and your gerbil is over and out. This creates at least two problems. First, the tiny fellow could be hurt by the fall, especially if the tank is sitting on a table several feet high. Secondly, if you also have a pet dog or cat, the gerbil will look like a plaything and be treated the same way. An ounce of prevention will save hours of regret.

For bedding, chlorophyll chips or cedar chips are suggested. Since gerbils are odorless, these chips will absorb the small amount of odor given off by their droppings. This way, the tank will have to be cleaned no more often than once a month. Also, since gerbils are determined chewers, they'll love to get their teeth into those chips. In a day, one inch of chips from the bag becomes two or more inches, thanks to the industry of your gerbils. They really go at it with a passion—holding a chip between front paws and chomping away, as if it were an ear of corn to eat or a harmonica to be played. And while they're at it, their expressions are priceless, as any gerbil-owner will tell you.

With chewers like these, expect anything you put in their tank to be worthy of their teeth's attention—and their enjoyment. They like a stick of wood, a piece of cloth to unravel, a cardboard roll from paper towels, shredded newspaper. Only metal and glass will survive, and that won't stop a gerbil from giving it everything he has. If he can get his teeth on it, any object is fun and worth a gnaw. But don't worry about your fingers—gerbils know the difference between people and things.

When a gerbil isn't eating or sleeping, he's ready to entertain himself—and you. And he doesn't mind being watched. The idea of shyness doesn't exist in the gerbil kingdom. Put an empty cardboard box in his tank and he'll hop right up to it. First he sniffs at this new thing. *No, it's not food*, he decides. So he jumps into it and scampers around, checking it thoroughly. *Okay, it's safe. Let's see. . .what should I use it for?*

Aha! He turns it on its side and fills it with chips. *Now that that's done, it's time to empty the old box, turn it over, and fill it again.* The box is soon sitting upside down like a square-backed turtle, while the gerbil builds tunnels in the chips underneath it. He sprints in and out, clambers on top of it, jumps off, clears away all the chips under it, piles them on the roof, brushes them away, and stuffs them back underneath.

If there are two gerbils, they'll get into a game of tag or hide-and-seek around the box, or labor together on a construction project. When you're a gerbil, life is work, work is play, and it's always satisfying—for him and you.

Finally, your gerbils will get tired of the idea of a whole box. In a day or two, what was a four-sided playground will be bite-sized snippets of cardboard well-mixed with the chips.

Gerbils are vegetarians, and subsist happily on a dry mixture of grains and seeds. They can be fed commercially packaged mixes (sometimes labeled hamster food), dry cereal and bird seed, shelled peanuts, dry dog food, and sunflower seeds. If you prefer to give them one diet exclusively, make it the packaged mix or dog food. Each of these will provide a complete, balanced diet and will keep your gerbils healthy. Like most animals, gerbils are not concerned about variety in their food and will never be bored by an unchanging diet.

However, you may get bored and want to feed them different things. That's fine—just be sure that their diet is balanced. Dry cereal or popcorn are acceptable treats for gerbils, but they are not healthy as a steady diet. A properly fed gerbil will never behave listlessly or lose patches of fur. If either of those things happen, you're seeing signs of poor nutrition, a warning to change his diet right away.

Gerbils generally eat about a tablespoon of food a day. If it is more convenient for you to feed them every other day, simply give them twice the amount a once-a-day feeder would. Unlike such animals as dogs, they will not overeat no matter how much food is placed in their tank. Put the food in a small dish or directly on the tank floor; they'll be satisfied either way. When you're dealing with gerbils, food placed in a dish tends to end up on the tank floor anyway. Sometimes, depending on his mood, the gerbil may cover the dish with wood chips. This might be his way of hiding it or storing it for tomorrow. In any case, while people like their food neatly set in a dish, gerbils don't care.

Your furry pets are apt to be as individual in their taste for treats as humans. Some gerbils like apples or celery, but others don't. The authors' gerbils adore raw carrots, but whether for the carrots' water content or for their crunchiness we do not know. So try different hard fruits or vegetables and see which your gerbils will eat and which they'll refuse.

Since their native habitat is the desert, gerbils do not require much water. A water bottle—glass, not plastic—with a tube attached to the stopper can be attached to the side of a gerbil cage or hung from the top of a tank. The tube, bent at an angle, allows a gerbil to suck out drops of water as needed. These water bottles are sold at any pet shop.

You may be wondering why you couldn't fill a dish with water and place that in the gerbil's tank. Well, if you did, you'd find that it would be overturned quickly, or be loaded with wood chips that form a soggy mess.

Don't worry if your gerbils seem to be drinking very little so long as they are healthy and active. And, if you provide raw carrots, don't be surprised if they snub the water bottle entirely: the carrot contains water. Even so, make sure that they are always supplied with water, particularly in warm weather.

Nobody has ever scientifically tested the intelligence of a gerbil, but everyone who has owned one knows what bright creatures they are. If a human is gentle with a gerbil, the animal will repay him with trust and friendliness. Taming one is simple. Put your hand in his tank and let him sniff it. After you've done that two or three times, and the gerbil knows that you're a friend, he'll run right over to your hand—unless he's busy eating, playing, or sleeping.

The next time you put food in the tank, keep your hand near it. As the gerbil investigates, then starts to eat, gently stroke his back with a finger. He will begin to associate your hand with good things and accept your touch at non-feeding times.

To lift him out of the tank, grab a gerbil by the tail—the closer to his body, the better. It will not hurt him to be lifted that way, though he'll squirm and try to figure out what's happening. Then, cup him gently but firmly in your other hand, without letting go of his tail. When he seems calm and secure, you may let go of the tail and begin stroking him or softly scratching his head and back.

Soon he may be willing to take food from your hand, to sit in your pocket, or to crouch on your shoulder. But never forget that you are responsible for his safety, so be careful to insure that he doesn't fall—it's a long drop from a person's shoulder to the floor for a gerbil. Just keep a hand ready to catch him when he is perched on your shoulder or head.

Once you've tamed your gerbil, he will trust you completely and be your friend for life. He's an ideal pet—needing a minimum of care, while giving so much love and fun to his human master.

4

Water Animals

Keeping aquatic creatures as pets can be a simple and inexpensive hobby—or it can become as complex and costly as putting together a championship major league baseball team. Fish fanciers usually start out with the idea that it would be nice to have a small home aquarium. But once they dip their toes into the world of water animals, they are hooked for life.

Tropical fish

If you are interested in raising tropical fish, you should know a few basic facts. The first is, the number of fish you keep will depend on the size of the aquarium you provide for them. There is a simple rule of thumb to follow: for every inch of fish, there must be one gallon of water. Let's say you have a ten-gallon fish tank. If there is nothing else in it, it could hold almost ten gallons of water.

However, the equipment, plant life, pebbles, gravel and sand, and the like, which are needed to provide a proper environment, take up a certain amount of space. Because of that we will assume you now can put seven to eight gallons of water into the tank. Next, let's say that the fish you have chosen are about two inches long. This means you should not have more than four fish in the tank.

Does this mean that five fish in these conditions would die of overcrowding? Probably not. But raise the number to nine or ten fish and you're likely to face the problem most novice tropical-fish keepers encounter. Some of the little swimmers will die, due to insufficient oxygen in their environment.

Tropical fish are beautiful to watch.

The next basic fact to know is: some tropical fish will live together peacefully, but others will not. The person best able to advise you on this matter is a well-informed dealer in tropical fish. Caution: not all pet-shop owners are fish experts. It is best, therefore, to buy your fish in a store that specializes in tropical fish. The owner of this store could not stay in business very long if the fish he keeps are not healthy. Furthermore, his business depends on his customers' good will, so he will not give you bad advice. If the store owner says that two species you are selecting will not live together, take his word for it.

The third basic fact is: don't overcrowd the tank with plants. People decorate their aquariums with green growing things because they look nice and are good for the fish. And they *do* make the fish tank look like a miniature underwater world. Too many plants, however, can make it impossible for you to see the fish. But even more important, overplanting will deprive the fish of oxygen. And, if they can't get enough oxygen, they'll die. (A more complete explanation of plants and oxygen is given in the section on goldfish.)

Why should a tank holding tropical fish have any plants at all? Aside from the natural beauty of the setting, the plants serve to block out excess light. The plants also serve as spawning places for many varieties of tropical fish. Of course, if your fish spawn successfully, you may need a second fish tank to avoid overpopulation in the original tank. . .and that's how tropical-fish fanciers become hooked by their hobby.

Tropical fish are so-called because they come to this country from different tropical areas around the world. They are warm-water animals. This means that your tank's temperature should be maintained at about 75° Fahrenheit. Some species require higher temperatures, while other species require temperatures lower than 75°. Again, you'll have to rely on your fish expert to tell you the appropriate temperature for the fish you favor. In all cases, tropical-fish tanks must be electrically heated.

Sunlight is the worst possible source of heat for a fish tank. When the sunlight strikes the water, it will raise the temperature far too high. Then, at night, the lack of sunlight will cause the temperature to drop too low. Tropical fish need a constant temperature, not one that goes from boiling to freezing, or that even varies a few degrees either way.

In addition, sunlight will cause aquarium plants to grow too rapidly. This is fine for the plants but miserable for the fish, whose living space will shrink as the plants grow larger and larger. So an aquarium must be kept in a spot where no direct sunlight will reach it.

The next important fact of tropical-fish keeping is that overfeeding kills fish. This is not because they overeat, but because rotting, uneaten food ruins the quality of the water. Your local tropical-fish expert can tell you what food and how much food your species requires.

Beyond that, you must not forget that the water should be filtered constantly for it to remain clean. This requires an automatic pump-and-filter system, which will circulate the water, keeping the temperature the same in all parts of the tank. It also aerates the water, supplying the fish with enough oxygen. Finally, it filters out bits of uneaten food, dust, and other unwanted matter, to a certain extent. You will still have to remove fish droppings and uneaten food that settle to the floor of the tank, and for that you'll need a siphon system. All of this equipment is available at tropical-fish shops.

Unless you are prepared for the costs that come with starting a tropical-fish aquarium and maintaining it properly from then on, you are better off selecting a less difficult and expensive water pet. With this in mind, we recommend two interesting and attractive water animals: the goldfish and the seahorse.

Goldfish

Among popular pets the goldfish ranks near the top of the list. To the Chinese of 3,000 years ago, who first kept them as pets, the goldfish meant good luck. Maybe the goldfish *was* lucky, because it can live as long as 100 years if properly fed and housed. That's right—this small, colorful fish, an offshoot of the wild carp, can survive for an entire century! Let's look at the little swimmer's history.

The wild carp was a dull green or brown fish which lived in fresh-water lakes and ponds, and was used by man as a food fish. Its only real distinction was that it could live a long life. But, every once in a while, a red or reddish-gold one was born. The beauty of it, as it swam among its plainer cousins, impressed those who saw it so much that they agreed it was too rare and beautiful to waste as food.

Also, being a member of a family with a life-span greater than man's made the goldfish even more precious. Soon, giving a pet goldfish to a friend came to be a high compliment. And by keeping one, the owner and his household were insuring that good luck would come to them.

By 1500 A.D. the hobby of keeping a pet goldfish in a garden pool or earthenware bowl was introduced into Japan, where it has remained popular ever since. Then, in 1692, the first pet goldfish were transported from the Orient to Europe. They reached England on a ship from Macao, a port in China. From England, where they scored an immediate success, goldfish were taken to the continent of Europe. And on the continent they were treated as very special pets, indeed. No royal palace was complete without a bowl of shimmering, glowing goldfish.

The first goldfish to set fin in the United States was transported here about 1859. We say "about" because that is the date when they are first mentioned as being in this country. From that time to now, this lovely and easily kept species has remained a standard, all-American pet. They may not bring a guarantee of long life to their keepers, but they still are marvelous pets.

Some people believe that goldfish are very delicate and hard to keep alive. These people say that they have had many goldfish, but that all of them died in a short time. This should not happen. Whenever it does, it is almost always because of one very wrong idea about goldfish.

These people believe, mistakenly, that the goldfish is a *tropical* fish, and so they put their shiny swimmers in warm water. The fact is, the goldfish is not tropical, and it lives best in water that feels quite cool to human touch.

How can you know what temperature of water is right for your pet? Simple. Fill a large pot with ordinary tap water, right from the kitchen faucet. Let it stand for a few hours or a day. The water will soon become room temperature. It is now just right for your goldfish. Of course, if you put your finger in the water, it will feel very cool. It may even seem much colder than the temperature in the room. But it really isn't. The water feels cool to you because your body temperature is 98.6° Fahrenheit, and the room temperature is more likely to be between 60° and 75° Fahrenheit.

If you intend to keep one or two goldfish, a standard glass goldfish bowl will be the right-sized house. Just put in the water, let it reach the proper temperature, add the goldfish, and you're all set.

Packaged goldfish food provides all the nutrients your pet needs, which makes feeding no problem whatever. Goldfish will not overeat, but dropping too much food in the bowl can harm them. Uneaten food falls to the bottom and begins to rot. If care isn't taken to keep the bowl clean, the water will turn cloudy, and the sides of the glass will become slimy. Like a polluted lake or river, the water will soon not contain enough oxygen for the fish to breathe. So too much food *can* kill a goldfish, even though the fish knows enough not to eat more than it needs.

A few grains of food every day, or every other day, will provide enough of a meal. And, if you feed your goldfish at the same time every day, you'll soon find that your pet knows its feeding time. Suppose you decide to feed it about five in the afternoon every day, and you follow that schedule for a period of time. Watch the goldfish in the morning. It swims around, seldom coming up to the surface of the water. Then, watch it at 4:30 P.M. or so. It dives to the bottom, noses around, swims to the surface, dives again, darts back and forth, comes up again. Like some energetic little athlete, it moves around quickly, endlessly.

Now, drop a few grains of food on the surface of the water. With a flip of his tail, your fish will swim to the food and start eating. To prove that this is more than a lucky accident, change the feeding schedule for a couple of days. Put the food into the bowl in the morning. Eventually, your fish may spot the food and come for it. But it is just as possible that the fish will follow the original schedule even though you don't.

There is no need for the stones, shells, ceramic castles, and other items which some people use to decorate a goldfish bowl. They certainly serve no purpose for the fish, and they can be harmful to its health. Unless these adornments are kept very clean, they are probably going to become covered with algae. When that happens, they look as if they are coated with a green or brown film and feel slimy to the touch. Like rotting food, this affects the quality of the water, reducing the amount of oxygen available to the goldfish.

And what about the custom of putting a layer of

sand on the bottom of the bowl? That's worst of all. Rocks and shells can be scrubbed with an old toothbrush, but have you every tried to scrub sand? No—the only sensible way to clean sand is by boiling it in a pot of water for a period of time long enough to kill the algae, straining and washing away all impurities, then putting it back in the bowl. As you can see, it's best to not use sand in the first place.

If you do want to put in a few stones, shells, or pieces of coral because they'll look nice, just make sure to treat them before putting them in the bowl. Treatment means a thorough scrubbing and boiling in water for at least an hour. This will kill and remove all trace of animal and plant life that might be dangerous to the fish. It will also remove any salt from a shell or coral branch that came from the ocean. Goldfish live in fresh water and cannot survive in salt water.

After the one-hour boiling treatment, be sure to keep your bowl ornaments clean by giving them regular scrubbings with a toothbrush and scouring powder, followed by a thorough rinsing with clean water. How often should this be done? Whenever it's time to change the water.

It is impossible to say whether the goldfish's water should be changed every two weeks, or three weeks, or once a month. That's because conditions vary too much from one home to the next. In general, however, you should plan on cleaning the bowl and changing the water once a month in the winter and twice a month in the summer. Some people, who insist on changing the water every few days, may be horrified at this. But they are probably the same people who

The stones and ferns in this goldfish bowl make an interesting arrangement, but they must be kept very clean or they will become covered with algae.

believe that goldfish are delicate tropical fish, and who have never had one last more than a few weeks.

The less you disturb your goldfish, the better. So, while you give it the proper amount of attention, don't become a fanatic about care. That is, don't kill it with kindness. Instead, just keep a watchful eye on the level of water in the bowl. When you see it has dropped more than a half-inch, change the water and bring it up to the right level. (The right level is just above the widest part of the bowl. This is usually two-thirds up the height of the bowl, measuring from the bottom to the top.) Another sign that it's time to change the water is when it is beginning to look dark or cloudy.

There are some things to do before you actually change the water. First, prepare a pot of tap water by filling the pot and allowing it to stand for a few hours, to reach room temperature. When it has reached the temperature of the old water in the bowl, it is ready. Now, put some of the fresh water in a jar, and transfer the fish to the jar. To do this, you may use a small fishnet with a handle, which is made for this purpose. Be very gentle.

Dump out all the old water and the ornaments. Scrub the bowl with scouring powder or detergent and rinse the glass under running water to remove all of the soap. Clean all the ornaments and set them back in the bowl. Then add the fresh water. Last of all, transfer your fish from the jar to its clean home. The fish and bowl will sparkle like new.

After you have done this cleaning a number of times, you should develop an accurate feeling for the

95

right water temperature. If this happens, you will not need to have the water stand around to reach the right temperature. You will be able to judge when the temperature of the water running from the tap is just what it should be for your pet's comfort and safety.

Because a goldfish is a cool-water fish, the bowl must never be placed in the sun. Not only will direct sunlight cause the water to heat too much, it will also speed up the growth of bacteria and algae that can choke off oxygen. Find a light—but not sunny—spot in the house, and stand the goldfish bowl there. Make sure the sun doesn't reach it another part of the day.

Plants which grow in water will certainly look very pretty in a goldfish bowl, but they are more trouble than they are worth. You may have heard that plants add oxygen to the water and use up carbon dioxide—balancing the effect of the fish, which uses oxygen and gives off carbon dioxide. This can be true, but under only one set of conditions. The process, which is call photosynthesis, depends on sunlight. In the absence of sunlight, plants will add no significant amount of oxygen to the water, and will use no carbon dioxide. And you can't keep your goldfish bowl in the sun, or it will kill the goldfish. So, it's obviously best to keep the bowl clear of plants.

If you have two goldfish, and even if you are absolutely certain that one is male and the other female, don't expect ever to see any young fish increase the bowl's population. Goldfish almost never reproduce in this sort of environment. For that to happen would require a large tank in which the conditions more closely resemble a goldfish's natural home. If you do enlarge your number of goldfish and put them in a tank, then breeding can occur.

When goldfish breed, the female will become swollen with eggs. Then, sometime between May and August, she will lay her 500-to-1,000 eggs in the water. As she is laying the eggs, the male will follow her around, fertilizing them. The fertilized eggs will hatch within eight or nine days. However, even if every egg is hatched (which is rare), it is unusual for more than a few of the baby fish to survive. Once more, nature is keeping things in balance.

People who have veiltail, bubble-eye, or other unusual varieties of goldfish are often disappointed after their exotic pets have bred. Two veiltail goldfish, with their glorious, shimmering fins and tail, are likely to produce plain old goldfish. Perhaps, if you're lucky, one or two of the offspring will look like their glamorous parents; but most of the babies will not. What is more, should one or two of the little ones be veiltails, a mating between them or between their children will probably produce just a lot of plain goldfish. But don't let it worry you, there's nothing wrong with your fish.

All of the exotic varieties of goldfish are freaks or mutations. This doesn't make them any less beautiful, of course. It does mean, however, that they are not truly new strains.

Here is an example of a true strain: if two Scottish Terriers are bred, they will produce only Scottish Terriers. And their puppies will grow into adults, mate with other Scottish Terriers, and produce more Scottish Terriers. So long as they are purebreds, the parents will always breed true to kind. The same is true of different breeds of dogs, or cats, or fish. The only exception to this rule is the freak or mutation, and that happens in all forms of life.

If you happen to be someone who likes the way a fancy goldfish looks, don't be discouraged from buying one. Just keep two things in mind. One, they can be very expensive. And two, remember that an ordinary goldfish, which costs very little, is exactly the same as the exotic fish, except for the bumpy head, bulging eyes, or long tail. And, if you do hope to breed fish, you'll end up with a tankful of ordinary goldfish after one, two, or three generations.

For our money, we'd take the plain old beautiful, luck-bringing variety of goldfish. As the ancient Chinese might have said, "May your golden swimmer bring you great happiness, and live to 100 years."

Seahorses

Imagine a creature that has the head of a horse, the pouch of a kangaroo, the tail of a monkey, the hard shell of an insect, eyes that move independently, and which lives in water. It may sound too fantastic to exist, but it does, and it's called a seahorse.

Seahorses don't look as if they should be called fish, but they are and they live in the oceans throughout the world. They can be found near the coastlines of every continent on earth, except for the shorelines of the polar regions. Of course, the easiest way for you to find them is by going to a pet store that has them in tanks.

There are about 20 species of seahorse in existence,

but only two of these are commonly kept as pets in America. These are (1) the dwarf seahorse, which would measure about two inches long if you could convince it to stretch out next to a ruler, and (2) the common seahorse, which can grow as long as ten inches. Actually, the variety of common seahorse usually sold in pet shops seldom grows to more than five-and-a-half inches, which makes it easier to keep in an aquarium.

The dwarf variety is really the best species of seahorse for anyone beginning his own home aquarium. It is inexpensive, doesn't need very much room, eats food which is easy to obtain, and it is not impossible to breed. Most important, even though all seahorses need to live in a salt-water environment, the dwarf is not fussy about the temperature of the water in his aquarium. Whatever temperature is maintained in your home will suit a seahorse. And if the salinity (the amount of salt in a given quantity of water) changes slightly, it will not hurt this adaptable pet. Of course, when a great amount of water evaporates from the bowl or tank, the extreme salinity that results may harm the seahorse. But it isn't hard to add fresh water to create a healthful balance again. As with goldfish, you just have to check on your pet's living conditions every so often.

The other requirements for keeping healthy seahorses are just as simple. First, prepare their home. You'll want to start with two—a male and a female— hoping that they will mate. Buy a large, deep fishbowl or a salt-water tank. The ordinary fish tank, used for fresh-water fish, must be specially treated if it is to be used. That is because of the metal parts of the tank. Salt water eats away metal much faster than fresh water, and that corrosion is harmful to seahorses. An old fresh-water tank can be made safe by painting all metal parts with aquarium cement. It comes in liquid form and isn't difficult to apply.

Nothing made of metal should be placed in a seahorse's home because of corrosion. Also unsuitable are shells, coral, and driftwood found on the beach. They may contain bits of matter (metal, plant, or animal) which would poison the aquarium water. These decorative items *can* be used—but only after they have been processed to remove any and all foreign matter. As you can see, it really is best to buy proper, safe tank decorations at the pet shop.

These decorations are more than nice-looking items as far as seahorses are concerned. They actually need objects in their tank. When they are swimming, these creatures are able to stay in a vertical (straight up) position by moving the fins on their backs. But when a seahorse stops, it must have something around which it can wrap its tail. A piece of standing coral or plastic is ideal for that purpose. And there is no way for a seahorse to eat food on the bottom of the tank unless there is something it can use as an anchor near the food. As with monkeys, the tail of a seahorse has a function—grabbing and holding onto objects. Indeed, a seahorse can starve in a tank full of food if it has nothing to hold itself near the food.

Seahorses eat only living organisms. They locate their food by sight, and suck it in as if feeding through an invisible straw. Newly hatched brine shrimp,

Seahorses use their tails to '"anchor" themselves in the water.

which can be bought at pet shops, make the best food for pet seahorses. That makes feeding no problem at all. Seahorses will eat brine shrimp from birth, and will never need a change of diet for their entire life-span.

Considering their size, seahorses are huge eaters, so you don't have to worry about overfeeding them. The pet shop owner can suggest what amount of brine shrimp to put into the tank, since he'll know the size of the tank and the number of seahorses you have. Then, observe your seahorses over a period of time. If they finish their food very quickly, increase the size of their daily meal. Just make sure that they have enough light in the tank. Seahorses will not eat in the dark or in very dim light. This is because, in nature, they are unable to see their prey at night. As a result, they have evolved into daytime feeders, or in conditions where there is enough light.

If you have a male and a female, you may get the chance to witness one of the most remarkable phenomena in the world—the breeding and birth of baby seahorses. Breeding can take place in spring, summer, and fall. The male does a sort of courtship dance, or swim, near the female. When both are ready to mate, they may entwine their tails, or both may grab onto a stick or piece or coral to keep them next to each other.

The male and female face one another. Then the female deposits fertilized eggs in the male's pouch. The father-to-be then carries the brood like a kangaroo.

Dwarf seahorses are born about ten days after fertilization. Other species of seahorse take longer— up to a month-and-a-half. When the babies are ready to emerge, a little one will poke his head out of Pop's pouch and wiggle his way out into the water. He'll swim up to the surface, gulp air to fill his swim bladder, and start eating shrimp brine immediately. One by one, his sisters and brothers—maybe as many as 25 of them—will follow. Each will be about one-half of an inch long and will be a perfect copy of the parents. In time, like babies of all kinds, they'll reach adult size.

In their ocean homes, seahorses are ready to breed within a week after father gives birth. But this seldom happens in an aquarium. As with many other animals, seahorses seem to know instinctively that overbreeding will lead to an impossibly overcrowded environment. So don't expect to see a big, bulging pregnant male seahorse in your tank too often.

In two months baby seahorses grow into adult size. But you can still tell that they are young by the cirri on their heads and bodies. Cirri are stiff, hairlike branches. They appear at about one month after birth and begin to get smaller after about six months. Sometimes they disappear completely. Why they grow to begin with and what purpose they serve is still a mystery to scientists. All that is known is that young seahorses have cirri, and that females are likely to have more than males.

The gentle little horse of the sea, with its proud, erect posture and pretty, curved tail, has a life-span of approximately two years in captivity. From the moment of birth, as you'll see, it will prove to be a charming, captivating pet.

5
Amphibians and Reptiles

Among the most misunderstood creatures in the animal kingdom are the amphibians and reptiles. In the reptile family, for example, snakes are sometimes thought of as being slimy and dangerous. The truth is, snakes have dry skins and most of them aren't in the least dangerous. It's the story of the serpent in the Garden of Eden that started the false idea that snakes are bad, but that's an unfair burden for all the snakes of the world to have to carry.

Frogs and Toads

Among the amphibians—animals that live in water and on land—frogs and toads also have been saddled with false reputations. For instance, how many times have you heard that touching a toad causes warts? That's plain silly. It came about because toads have bumpy skin and frogs have markings that look like warts, and in the past people didn't know that warts are caused by viruses.

How about the old saying that newts rain out of the

sky? That story seems to be based on the fact that these creatures come out of their hiding places in wet weather. But rainy skies don't produce newts any more than they produce cats and dogs.

The nonsense tales about these animals occasionally discourage some people from considering them as pets, which is sad. Especially when you get to know them and find that they are quite interesting, safe, easy to care for, hardy, and inexpensive.

Frogs and toads start life the same way, as eggs in a pond or lake. Both kinds of eggs hatch into tadpoles, then change into a frog or toad. It is almost impossible to tell a frog egg from a toad egg because they look just about the same. But there is a clue that might help you. Frog eggs are often laid in a cluster; toad eggs are laid in a long string. Of course, any sort of disturbance

Frogs always live in or near water.

in the water can change the arrangement of the eggs, making identification pretty tough.

Just to keep you guessing, even when the eggs have hatched into tadpoles you still won't be able to tell if you have a toad or a frog. In both species, the tadpole has gills for breathing, a tail for swimming, and looks more like a baby fish than anything else. But wait a few days and you'll see remarkable changes.

The tadpole will begin coming to the surface of the water to gulp air as its lungs develop and its gills close. Little hind legs will appear, then the forelegs, with the left leg usually popping out before the right leg. Soon the tail grows shorter and shorter, as it is absorbed into the body. Before the absorption of the tail begins tadpoles eat microscopic organisms that live in their pond or lake. However, as soon as the tail begins to shrink, the tadpole stops eating. What is happening is that the tail itself is providing all the nourishment the animal needs! And then, one day, you have a fully formed frog or toad. At last, you know what you have. . .if you know the differences between frogs and toads.

What are the differences? First of all, a frog's skin is fairly smooth and moist, whereas a toad's skin is usually dry and covered with wartlike bumps. On land, a frog moves in long leaps and jumps; a toad walks or takes short hops. A frog tends to be slender, with a long and narrow head; a toad has a pudgy body and a short, broad head. The final difference is that frogs live in or right near water at all times; toads get the moisture they need to live by squatting in puddles of water every now and then. What's more, toads are found in ponds and lakes only when it's time to mate.

There are many species of frogs and toads in the United States, and every one of them makes a good pet. Housing and feeding them are very simple matters. An empty fish tank is an ideal place in which to build a terrarium. If you are keeping a toad, the fish tank should contain a floor of loamy soil, a few medium-sized rocks, and some growing plants. A small dish of water will supply all the moisture your toad needs. If you are keeping a frog, the tank should be divided into two equal parts. Half will hold water, and half will be land. A board should be fitted snugly from one corner of the tank on a diagonal line to the opposite corner. This will divide the tank into two triangles. The board should be about three inches high. Also, since frogs can jump well, a wire mesh cover should be placed on top of its home in your house. The cover should be firmly attached to the tank, or weighted, so the frog won't jump up and knock it off.

Now, fill one of the triangular areas with stones, pebbles and gravel, to the height of the board. Pour water into the other triangular section, then place a few stones into this wet area so that they form a staircase leading to the top of the board. This will make it easy for your frog to go from land to water, and back again, whenever he wants to.

What do toads and frogs eat? All kinds of insects and worms, but only when they are alive. This doesn't mean you have to go out to dig in the ground or catch insects for your pet. Instead, satisfy the amphibian's hunger with a diet of raw chopped meat, bits of

107

Compared to frogs, toads have a "square" look.

hard-boiled egg, and commercially prepared food sold at any pet shop. Even though toads and frogs eat only live food in nature, they will adapt to this diet in captivity. Just make sure that both the food and water are kept fresh.

Frogs and toads live many years if they are treated properly. They require a warm environment, and normal room temperature will suit them quite well. Both frogs and toads hibernate, selecting a warm, dark place in the fish tank, and spending all the cold months there. (Even though they are indoors, they live by their internal clock.) So, don't worry if your pet begins to eat less and less as winter approaches. But, since you may not be sure if your pet is hibernating, put a little food near it. If the food isn't eaten in a few days, replace it with fresh food. There is nothing wrong with it; it's just getting ready for that long winter's nap. Next spring it will be up and about again, friendly and talkative. Or maybe "singative" would be a better word. Some people describe the sound of a frog or toad's voice as a croak. But that doesn't do justice to the voice of these four-legged animals. They chirp and croon, honk and boom, each one contributing an interestingly varied song to the chorus of nature. And being in an indoor tank won't discourage them from singing.

Salamanders and Newts

These are tailed amphibians. The two names can be used interchangeably, but salamander usually refers to the land species, while newt refers to the ones that live in water. Both can be found throughout the United States, and both make excellent pets. Like frogs and toads, they can be kept in a tank, with a small amount of water for salamanders, and half land and half water—remember those triangular sections—for newts. Both can be fed the same foods as frogs and toads, and they also go into hibernation each year. In fact, salamanders, newts, toads, and frogs can all live together in the same terrarium and be very happy.

The salamander (above) and the newts (below) are amphibians which go into hibernation each year.

Chameleons

Chameleons are not related to salamanders and newts, which are amphibians. The chameleon is a lizard, and a member of the reptile family. What does this mean? First of all, the eggs from which lizards hatch are laid in the soil, not in water. Lizards are land creatures throughout their life cycle. (Not all reptiles are land creatures. In fact, most of them—such as turtles, tortoises, and certain snakes—prefer the water. However, all reptiles have backbones and either creep or crawl on the land.)

Chameleons and their fellow lizards need a dry, warm terrarium, containing soil and greenery. Since they are cold-blooded, like the amphibians, they must have a controlled climate. And, like the amphibians, they hibernate every winter.

In nature lizards eat insects and some vegetation, depending on the species of lizard and what is available in the environment. In your home a balanced diet can consist of bits of raw meat, egg, fruit, and greens. There is no reason to remove uneaten food from a lizard's tank. In fact, it's a good idea to let a piece of ripe fruit sit in the terrarium. Flies and gnats attracted to it will become part of the lizard's menu as fast as you can say "lizard's tongue."

Of all the lizards on earth, none is more fascinating than the chameleon. Not only is it a healthy pet able to live for five years, it responds well to human attention and will come to know its master. Best of all, the chameleon has the amazing ability to change color to match its surroundings, when its mood changes, or

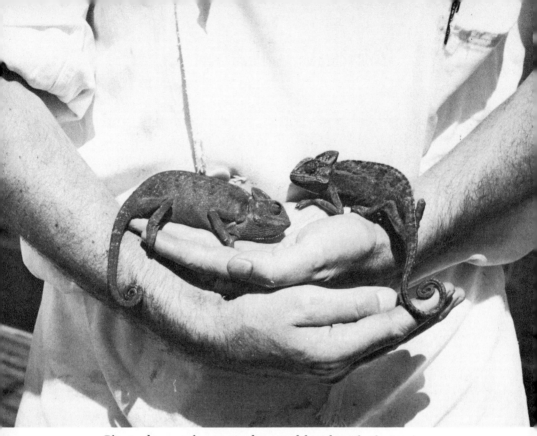

Chameleons change colors to blend with their environment.

when the temperature rises or falls.

This doesn't mean that a chameleon, placed on a plaid or polka-dot cloth, turns plaid or polka-dotted. But nature has supplied it with a built-in mechanism for camouflage. A chameleon on a brown twig will turn brown. Put it on a green leaf and soon the brown gives way to green. When a chameleon is cold, it will become a blotchy or pale yellow-gray. Increase the temperature and it will become its normal light green with a white belly. All of these qualities make the chameleon six inches (including a lo-o-ng tail) of fun and surprise for any pet lover.

Snakes

America's snakes come in a large variety, and only four types are dangerous to humans. These are the rattlesnake, coral, pigmy rattlers, and water moccasins. Even though you are unlikely to encounter one of these, and even though you know that a snake will not attack unless it feels threatened, you should never handle or approach any snake unless it has been identified for you.

How can safe snakes be recognized? By their color or markings. A safe snake is solid colored—green, dark blue, bluish-gray, or black—or has one or more long, straight stripes down its entire length. These colors and markings are guarantees of harmlessness. However, there are safe snakes which look similar to poisonous ones, so unless a herpetologist (a reptile expert) or some other well-informed person tells you it's harmless, keep your distance.

All of the harmless varieties of snakes make good pets. These cold-blooded animals require nothing more than a warm environment, tender handling, and a diet high in protein. In the wild, snakes eat live food, but will adjust to a menu of non-living things in your home. Raw meat, fish, and eggs are fine, along with a small dish of water. In cold weather snakes hibernate, and can last until the spring on one meal. For that matter, they don't eat too much in the warm months, going for a week to ten days between meals.

Snakes also are undemanding about their living quarters. A fish tank or a wooden box, with a dirt floor in either one, is a good place to keep snakes. Just be certain that your long, thin friend isn't exposed to direct sunlight, which can harm him. Normal room temperature and some shade are ideal conditions.

A snake that is comfortable, well-fed, and handled with gentleness will accept you as a friend. It will allow you to pick it up, drape it over your shoulder, and will curl up in your lap. Take good care of it and your grateful, silent snake will provide you with many days of charming and hypnotic pleasure. Why do we say hypnotic? Just stare into a snake's eyes, and you'll see why.

This is an Eastern garter snake—a harmless species.

Turtles and Tortoises

Of all the animals in the reptile-amphibian category, turtles and tortoises are usually the most easily acquired and the most commonly domesticated. Indeed, for anyone who wants to keep pets but has little experience, there is no better choice for a beginner than these easy-to-please, simple-to-care-for animals.

You don't know the difference between a turtle and a tortoise? First of all, there are at least three answers to that question.

In America, the popular notion is that turtles live mainly in water while tortoises live mainly on land. In Great Britain, however, the word "tortoise" refers to some species that live on land and some that live in water. A third answer is the definition that tortoises are those with high, domed shells, and turtles have flatter shells.

The fact is, even scientists who specialize in studying reptiles (turtles and tortoises are forms of reptiles) cannot agree on which is which. So there you are—just about where you were at the beginning. For that reason, let's agree to use the word "turtle" to refer to these animals who carry their homes around with them.

While it is true that some of the more than 250 species live in deserts where there is almost no water, and some live in the ocean, all turtles need some of the same basic conditions to survive. One is air, because all turtles are air breathers. Then what makes it possible for them to stay underwater for days?

Because, before submerging, the turtle takes a huge gulp of air. It's really huge because he has special muscles which pull the body organs away from his lungs, creating a larger-than-normal space for air.

The turtle then submerges. If he stays on the bottom of the pond and doesn't move around much, his air supply can last for days. But if the turtle is active—swimming around in search of food or for some other reason—the air will be used up more quickly.

Every species also needs a fairly steady temperature. Like other reptiles, turtles are not able to keep a constant body temperature, no matter how cold or warm the air may be. (Most animals, such as man, have a body temperature which never varies more than a couple of degrees in any kind of weather. For example, our normal temperature is about 98.6° Fahrenheit; a dog's normal temperature is about 101° Fahrenheit.) So, if you leave a turtle in very cold water, its body temperature will drop drastically and it may die. For the same reason, a turtle may die if it cannot escape from a hot midday sun in midsummer.

To keep their bodies at the right temperature— about 70 to 80°—turtles move from place to place. In areas where the temperature drops below freezing, some species burrow under the ground in winter. Once they are in their burrows, hibernating turtles live off the nourishment their bodies have stored during the warm months. And they will sleep contentedly in their burrows until spring warms the ground around them, which isn't a bad way to spend a freezing winter.

Turtles that live in hot desert regions, as a number

of species do, burrow into the ground to keep cool. This keeps them underground during the day, and they come up to the surface at night. Nevertheless, they are not considered nocturnal animals. While they may spend a good portion of the day inactive and underground and surface to feed in the early morning and late afternoon, they also may spend whole days above ground if the weather is cool enough.

One of the reasons people sometimes are unsuccessful at keeping turtles as pets is that they fail to meet the turtles' needs for temperature change. Let's take the common case of the glass bowl new turtle owners buy as housing for their pets. Such a bowl is not good because there isn't enough room in it to create a proper environment.

The best housing for a small turtle, bought at a pet shop, is a fish tank or a large, sturdy box. It is important to remember that a turtle needs dry land for burrowing and sunning, as much as it needs water. The box or tank can be made into a terrarium, providing just the right balance of water and land to keep the turtle in tip-top shape.

To create a small pool for your hard-backed friend, you can use a metal or plastic bowl. It should be deep enough to allow the turtle to swim freely and to be completely submerged. If you have in mind to buy a young turtle sold in pet shops, a bowl with a depth of two to four inches will be fine. Remember that the water must be changed regularly. That is, when it looks cloudy or dirty, change it. Even if it looks clean, changing it every three or four days is a good idea.

117

Set the bowl at one end of the box, then fill the rest of the box with loose, clean, sandy soil until it reaches the level of the top of the bowl. Now use some small rocks to build steps in the bowl and a patio where the turtle may sun itself. The rock steps make it possible for the turtle to get out of the pool anytime it's ready to stretch out in the sun. Arrange them in a gently sloped path from the bottom of the bowl up to a flat rock at the top.

A nice flat patio-rock for sunning helps to keep a turtle healthy. Turtles get vitamin D from sunlight, just as we humans do. Furthermore, scientists have learned that turtles use the heat and drying qualities of the sun to keep themselves free of algae, fungus, and parasites. So set the terrarium in a location that will allow about one to two hours of morning or late afternoon sunlight to fall on the sunning rock. But don't forget that midday sunlight can be too strong, especially in the summer months. As the seasons change, it will probably be necessary for you to shift the tank around, so that the sunlight will shine in the same place.

There is an easy way to find a good, basic location for your turtle's terrarium. Locate a place in the house where there is direct sunlight in the winter at about ten o'clock in the morning or three o'clock in the afternoon. It would be near a window that faces east or southwest. Make sure that the spot gets at least one full hour of sunlight, but is in shade at noon. Set your terrarium in place, with your turtle inside.

Now settle down and watch what your pet does. Pretty soon you'll see him climb onto the sun-bathed rock and sprawl across it. He'll stretch out his head and limbs, extending all of his claws. Then he'll simply lie there, as if taking a snooze. Actually, what is taking place is a necessary part of nature's design for turtles. The folds of his skin and the spaces between his claws are places where parasites might cling. And the shell surrounding his body can easily be softened by algae that accumulate in water— something that is definitely not good for a turtle. But that's why you have built him a sunning rock. Lying in the sun dries out all the breeding places for those

Turtles are popular and nondemanding pets.

microscopic creatures that might harm him. The sunlight also keeps him warm.

If a turtle is housed where it can reach water for cooling, a sunning rock for warming, and a dry soil area for burrowing (soil provides warmth in winter and coolness in summer), it can live a very long time.

Feeding a pet turtle is no problem. There was a time when people believed that turtles lived mainly on insects, and if that were true it could be difficult to feed a turtle in the house. However, it has been learned that plant life is really the major part of the diet of most species of turtles. Which means a pet turtle should be fed a selection of salad greens, some raw meat, and commercial turtle food. This will provide a balanced diet. For greens, a piece of raw spinach or the outer leaves of romaine lettuce will do the trick. To complete the meal, add a few bits of raw hamburger and a few grains of turtle food. Drop the leaf into the pool; the rest of the meal may be placed in the pool or in a small glass or plastic dish next to the pool. Try both ways and see which gets better results.

However much food your turtle eats in a half-hour is the right amount to give him. Watch what he eats because any food that isn't consumed in a reasonable time should be removed from the tank. That's because spoiled meat can do more harm to a turtle than if he missed a meal. The spinach or lettuce leaf in the pool of water does not have to be removed if it isn't eaten quickly; it won't spoil so soon. But it is still wise to replace it with a fresh leaf after a full day to prevent the buildup of algae in the water.

Don't worry about underfeeding your pet. Turtles

are not huge eaters. In summer a young turtle will usually eat every day and an older turtle may eat every other day. But then, in the fall, it's quite normal for any turtle to eat no more than once or twice a week. And as fall turns into winter, he'll eat even fewer meals, perhaps no more than once a week. Some turtles do not bother with food for several weeks during the winter, behaving as if they are in hibernation. Nature is telling him what to do.

So if your turtle refuses to come to the table, don't leap to the conclusion it is ill. Just offer a small amount of food every day, and it will be eaten when the turtle is ready for it. Also remember that cold conditions turn off a turtle's appetite. Keep the pool water about 75° Fahrenheit, and a turtle that stopped eating when the water was cooler may begin to eat again. Another wintertime tip: an overhead aquarium light will provide needed warmth.

In recent years many people have come to believe turtles should not be kept as pets. This followed the discovery that salmonella, a form of bacteria often found in spoiled food, can be transmitted by turtles. But have no fear—there is no danger if you follow sensible rules of hygiene and if you keep your turtle in a proper environment. First: *always* wash your hands right after handling a turtle or anything in his bowl or tank. This is a sensible rule to follow no matter what kind of pet you own.

Second: be certain that your turtle has enough sunlight, fresh food, and a clean home. A turtle that is sick or can make you sick is almost always one not kept in healthful conditions. Harmful bacteria will grow on meat left in a bowl too long. Since the turtle cannot remove the meat from his bowl, the pet owner must do it. It is your responsibility. And you also are responsible for seeing to it that there is a sunshiny place for the turtle to dry itself to prevent fungus from growing on its shell and to stay warm.

If you forget to change the water in the pool for a few days, or if the location of the bowl has become too cool, correct those conditions immediately. It's also a good idea to mix a tablespoon of salt with a gallon of water, then put the turtle in it for an hour. The salt-water mixture will help to kill any fungus that might have built up on its body.

Best of all, keep your turtle in a clean, sunny, warm home with fresh water and fresh food. That way you will prevent any problems from occurring. And don't forget—your cleanliness is important, so wash your hands as soon as you finish taking care of your turtle.

Baby turtles, sold in department stores and other places, often have a painted carapace. (The top of a turtle's shell is called a carapace, and the bottom is called a plastron.) The paint should be removed. To do this, scrape it off with the dull side of a knife blade (or other safe tool), taking care not to gouge the shell or cut yourself. If the paint is not removed, the turtle will not be able to grow. Just as birds molt (periodically lose their feathers and grow new ones), turtles shed the outer layers of the carapace and plastron as they grow.

Once a shell has grown on a turtle, the shell's size remains the same. The shell itself cannot continue to grow after it has formed around the turtle's body. But the turtle continues to grow, which means that it has to have a new, larger shell to hold its larger body. For this reason, the turtle must shed its too-small shell and replace it with a roomier one. The turtle gets rid of the old shell in the way a person rids himself of a house that has become too old to live in.

Two turtles in a home bowl or tank will live together very happily. But, even if you are sure that one is male and the other female, don't expect them to produce baby turtles. It almost never happens with turtles not living in a natural environment. However, if you find turtle eggs (at a pond, for instance), it is sometimes possible to get them to hatch. Turtles lay their eggs in sandy soil, after first scooping away some of the ground to form a hole. Once the eggs are laid in the hole, the female covers the eggs with soil and leaves them for nature to take its course. If no predator bird or animal finds them, they are likely to hatch, adding to the turtle population.

It is the location in which the eggs are laid that is most important. They are always deposited in a sunny spot, near water. These conditions keep the soil moist and warm. The sun warms the sand around the eggs, and the moisture keeps the shells from drying and cracking. The egg itself contains almost all yolk. This gives a newborn turtle enough fat to live on for a long time after birth.

If you find turtle eggs and want to try hatching them, start with a large, empty tin can. Wash it, then punch some small holes in the bottom. Next, fill the can part way with sandy soil. The best soil to use would be some from the same place where you found the eggs. Now, gently put the eggs on the soil, and cover them with more soil. Place the can in a pan of water until the soil is clearly wet, then set the can in a warm, sunny place, covering the top with a piece of burlap. After a day or two, when the sand has started to dry, give the can another soaking and put it back in the sun. Continue to do this until the eggs hatch.

Turtle eggs are laid in the spring and early summer. They hatch in late summer or fall. The length of time you will have to wait before your turtle eggs hatch cannot be predicted exactly. It will depend on the species of turtle and when the eggs were laid. Be patient, give the eggs a proper environment, and the chances are good that, in time, you will be rewarded with a family of tiny turtles!

Index

125

INDEX

127

THE AUTHORS

Francene and Louis Sabin are prolific authors, sometimes writing in collaboration and sometimes individually. They have written many books for Putnam's, one of the most popular being the longtime best-selling *Dogs of America*. The Sabins and their son make their home in Milltown, New Jersey, where they have enjoyed some of the "perfect pets" they discuss in this book.